ENGLISH-BULGARIAN
PHRASE BOOK

ENGLISH-BULGARIAN
PHRASE BOOK

- **More than 5,000 words and phrases**
- **Mini-dictionary**

HERMES PUBLISHERS

ENGLISH-BULGARIAN PHRASE BOOK

ISBN 954–26–0078–X

Hermes Publishers Head Office
59 Bogomil Street
Plovdiv 4000
Bulgaria
Tel. + 359 32 630 630
E-mail:info@hermesbooks.com

For order enquiries: please contact Customer Services Department at:
Tel: + 359 32 608 109
Fax: + 359 32 608 199

You can also visit us at: www.hermesbooks.com

Contents

Dear Reader,

This phrase book has been designed as a reliable guide through the many situations you are likely to encounter when travelling in Bulgaria. The material has been compiled and arranged so as to provide you with the most frequently used phrases in a given context, allowing you at the same time to construct your own sentences.

Every page is structured in three columns, with the transliteration of the Bulgarian words and phrases given in *Italics*. Stressed syllables in Bulgarian words and phrases are indicated by the symbol (') before them.

The English-Bulgarian dictionary at the end of the phrase book allows you quick reference and bridges the gap between the two languages.

The Pronunciation Notes and the Crash Course in Bulgarian Grammar provide guidelines to the basics of Bulgarian language.

And the useful insights into Bulgarian lifestyle and history will help you to easier understand this culture and make new friends.

Have a great time in Bulgaria!

Abbreviations used in the phrase book:

sg singular
pl plural
m masculine
f feminine
n neutral

BULGARIA AT A GLANCE

Official name	Republic of Bulgaria
Land area	110,994 sq km (42,855 sq mi)
Capital and largest city	Sofia (1,200,000)
Other major cities	Plovdiv; Varna; Burgas
Major physical features	
Elevation extremes	Highest point – Mt. Musala 2,925 m (9,594 ft). Lowest point – sea level along coast.
Climate	Temperate: cold, damp winters and hot, dry summers. January: -2 C° (28 F); July: 21 C° (69 F)
People	
Population	(July 2002 est) 7,621,337
Official language	Bulgarian
Religious affiliations (1998)	Bulgarian Orthodox 83,8%; Muslim 12,1%; Roman Catholic 1,7%; others 2,4%
Economy	
GDP (2002 est)	$50.6 billion
Industries	Electricity, refined petroleum, nuclear fuel, chemical products, machinery and equipment, base metals; food, beverages and tobacco
Currency	1 Bulgarian lev = 100 stotinki
Exchange rate	1 EUR = 1.955 BGL
Form of government	Parliamentary republic
Education and health	
Literacy (2002)	98%
Life expectancy (2002)	Males: 67.98 years Females: 75.22 years

Bulgaria – Past and Present

There's an old legend narrating that God summoned all the peoples on earth to give each a piece of nature's beauty. Every people had its share of God's creation. It so happened that Bulgarians turned up late and there was no earthly beauty left for God to give them. So God presented them with a piece of Heaven...

Situated in South-Eastern Europe, in the heart of the Balkan peninsula, Bulgaria can boast a unique combination of breathtaking high mountains, luscious valleys, azure sea and fine white sands. Together with the temperate climate, this unrivalled scenery makes the country ideal for both summer and winter tourism. The 13-century turbulent history of its people, marked with great upheavals, only turns Bulgaria into an even more exciting place to visit.

The old state of Bulgaria was established in 681 AD by the Bulgars – a Turkic people – and the Slavs. In the 9th century, the Thessaloniki brothers Cyril and Methodius created the Slavonic script (later known as the Cyrillic alphabet) that was to lay the foundation for great literary and cultural achievements. Overrun by the Ottoman Turks in 1393, the country was in a state of non-existence for almost five hundred years, but regained its independence in 1878. After World War II, Bulgaria entered the Eastern Communist Block. In November 1989, however, the totalitarian regime was overthrown and since then the country has been undergoing democratic changes which, hopefully, will soon reestablish Bulgaria as a part of united Europe.

Republic of Bulgaria

Vidin
Montana
Vratsa
Pleven
Lovech
Ruse
Silistra
Razgrad
Shumen
Târgovishte
Dobrich
Balchik
Albena
Varna
Zlatni pyasâtsi
Kamchia
Veliko Târnovo
Dryanovski manastir
Gabrovo
Troyan
Troyanski manastir
Sofia
Pernik
Karlovo
Koprivshtitsa
Hisarya
Sliven
Yambol
Nesebâr
Slânchev bryag
Pomorie
Burgas
Sozopol
Dyuni
Primorsko
Tsarevo
Ahtopol
Kyustendil
Borovets
Stara Zagora
Pazardzhik
Plovdiv
Rilski manastir
Blagoevgrad
Velingrad
Asenovgrad
Bachkovski manastir
Haskovo
Pamporovo
Smolyan
Kârdzhali
Sandanski

Map Legend

- capital
- major city
- town
- spa centre
- monastery
- summer resort
- winter resort

PRONUNCIATION NOTES

When talking about Bulgarian, one could say that, unlike English, what you speak is what you write. You will find most Bulgarian sounds familiar and the transliteration used in the phrase book will enable you to make yourself perfectly understood.

Below is the transliteration adopted in this phrase book:

а	a	п	p
б	b	р	r
в	v	с	s
г	g (as in gut)	т	t
д	d	у	u
е	e	ф	f
ж	zh (as **s** in treasure)	х	h
з	z	ц	ts (as in pan**ts**)
и	i	ч	ch (as in **ch**op)
й	y	ш	sh (as in **sh**op)
к	k	щ	sht (as in A**sht**on)
л	l	ъ	â
м	m	ь	
н	n	ю	yu (as in **u**niversity)
о	o	я	ya (as in **ya**rn)

NB! When the syllable border falls between *z|h* and *s|h*, they are divided by means of a hyphen so as not to be confused with the sounds *zh* and *sh*.

Vowels

While in Old Bulgarian there were 11 vowels, Modern Bulgarian has only six: **а** (as in f**a**ther), **ъ** (as in Oakl**a**nd), **о** (as in h**o**t), **у** (as in l**oo**k), **е** (as in p**e**n), **и** (as in p**i**n). They are of medium length, while the English vowels can be short and long. When stressed, Bulgarian vowels are clearly and distinctly pronounced. If in an unstressed position, they are not so clear and the wide vowels sound almost identical with the narrow ones.

Consonants

There are 39 consonants in Modern Bulgarian, which correspond to 21 letters. They are quite similar in pronunciation to the English consonants. The majority of Bulgarian consonants (except **л**, **м**, **н**, **р**, **й**, **х**) fall into two large categories, known as voiced and voiceless consonants:

Voiced Consonants	*Voiceless Consonants*
б	п
в	ф
г	к
д	т
ж	ш
з	с
дж	ч
дз	ц

It's worth noting that, when in a certain position (usually at the end of the word), voiced consonants become voiceless:

town	*grat*	град
enemy	*vrak*	враг
garage	*ga'rash*	гараж
sunset	*'zales*	залез

Although not typical for the Bulgarian language, there's sometimes an accumulation of two or more consonants, which usually leads to one of the consonants being dropped for the sake of easier pronunciation:

newspaper	*'vesnik*	вестник
actress	*ar'tiska*	артистка

Stress

Stress in Bulgarian is not fixed – it can practically fall on every syllable:

'маса
кра'сив
про'зорец
капи'тан

Stress in the phrase book is signified by the symbol (') before the stressed syllable.

Prepositions, conjunctions and contracted pronouns have no stress of their own and are usually pronounced together with the word they precede or come after.

Crash Course in Bulgarian Grammar

Bulgarian language belongs to the group of South Slavonic languages. Modern Bulgarian is the descendant of the oldest Slavonic literary language, Old Bulgarian. Modern Bulgarian has much in common with the other Slavonic languages, including noun gender as well as the finite/non-finite aspect of the verb opposition, which indicates the way a verb relates to time. Though sharing many of these characteristics, Bulgarian has some unique, "Balkan" features that distinguish it from the other Slavonic languages. In the course of its development, Bulgarian abandoned case system and turned to prepositions instead. It also adopted specific articles (contracted forms of the Old Bulgarian demonstrative pronouns, now attached immediately after the noun) and ways of forming comparative and superlative degree of adjectives. These features, among others, make Bulgarian quite a challenge, nevertheless, a rewarding one.

Nouns

Bulgarian nouns fall into 3 genders: masculine, feminine and neutral. Ancient people regarded everything in nature as having a "soul", and so they ascribed "gender" to men and women, plants and animals, geographical sites and abstract ideas.

Gender in Bulgarian is usually defined by the word's ending. Generally, nouns that end in a consonant, including the semi-vowel **й**, are masculine:

brother	*brat*	брат
end	*kray*	край

Nouns ending in **-а/я** are feminine:

mother	*'mayka*	майка
aunt	*'lelya*	леля

Nouns ending in **-o/-e** are neutral:

child	*de'te*	дете
village	*'selo*	село

The most common ending that signifies plural for masculine and feminine nouns is **-и**, which is added to the word (as the English **-s**: girl – girls):

teachers	*u'chiteli*	учители
tickets	*bi'leti*	билети
women	*zhe'ni*	жени
rooms	*'stai*	стаи

The usual ending in plural for neutral nouns is **-а** or **-я**, which replaces the final vowel:

beds	*leg'la*	легла
flowers	*tsve'tya*	цветя

Adjectives

Adjectives get the gender and number of the noun they modify.

Bulgarian adjectives have comparative and superlative degree. The comparative degree is formed when we put the particle **по-** before the noun: красив – по-красив (beautiful – more beautiful).

Likewise, when we put the particle **най-** before the adjective, we form the superlative degree: красив – най-красив (beautiful – the most beautiful).

Article

There's no indefinite article in Bulgarian. Its function is performed by the cardinal numbers **един** *(m)*, **една** *(f)*, **едно** *(n)*. The definite article is added to the end of the noun, and every gender has a definite article of its own. Masculine nouns get the definite article **-ът/-ят** (when the noun acts as the subject in the sentence) and **-а/-я** in all other cases. It's worth noting that in speech the **т** in **-ът/-ят** is usually omitted:

the man	*mâ'zhât*	**мъжът**

Feminine nouns get the definite article **-та**:

the woman	*zhe'nata*	**жената**

Neutral nouns get the definite article **-то**:

the child	*de'teto*	**детето**

In plural, masculine and feminine nouns get the definite article **-те**, which is added to the plural:

the men	*mâ'zhete*	**мъжете**
the women	*zhe'nite*	**жените**

Neutral nouns get the definite article **-та**:

the flowers	*tsve'tyata*	**цветята**

Pronouns

Personal pronouns in Bulgarian have both full and short forms. When acting as the subject in a sentence, personal pronouns are often omitted because this information is conveyed by the inflexion of the verb, which is specific for every person and number. Like many other languages, Bulgarian distinguishes between the familiar form of address, expressed by the pronoun **ти** (*ti*), and the more formal **вие** (*vie*) for 2nd person plural. Apart from the more formal circumstances, Bulgarians are quick to abandon **вие** and move directly to **ти**. Where not indicated, the most appropriate form of address in the given context is used in the phrase book.

Personal Pronouns

Singular

1. I	*as*	**аз**
2. you	*ti*	**ти**
3. he, she, it	*toy, tya, to*	**той, тя, то**

Plural

1. we	*'nie*	ние
2. you	*'vie*	вие
3. they	*te*	те

Possessive Pronouns

Apart from having specific forms for each person, possessive pronouns in Bulgarian (as well as adjectives) take the gender and number of the noun they modify.

Reflexive Pronouns

Bulgarian has only one reflexive pronoun for each personal pronoun: **се**. Besides the fact that it might refer to any subject, the personal pronoun can also mean "each other".

I wash **myself**.	Мия **се**.
They love **each other**.	Обичат **се**.

Verbs

Bulgarian verbs have no infinitive. The verb's basic form is the form for 1st person singular (this is the way verbs are given in the dictionary accompanying the phrase book). The most common verb inflexion is **-а/-я, -ам, -ям**. The person is expressed, primarily, in inflexions and, secondarily, by personal pronouns. Since the verb form has a specific inflexion for each person and number, personal pronouns are usually omitted.

Bulgarian verbs fall into 3 verb classes. The verb class is indicated by the ending of the verb in 3rd person sg. Present Tense:

– **е**	to write	*'pisha*	пиша
	he/she writes	*'pishe*	пиш**е**

– **и**	to think	*'mislya*	мисля
	he/she thinks	*'misli*	мисли
– **а**	to draw	*ri'suvam*	рисувам
	he/she draws	*ri'suva*	рисува

Present Tense

to write

Singular	*Plural*
1. пиша	пишем
2. пишеш	пишете
3. пише	пишат

The negative forms of verbs are formed with the negative particle **не** (no) put before the verb:

пиша/не пиша
работя/не работя

Future Tense

Future forms of Bulgarian verbs are formed by adding the particle **ще** (will) before the verb. Negative future forms are formed with **не ще/няма да** (will not) before the verb.

Singular	*Plural*
1. ще пиша	ще пишем
2. ще пишеш	ще пишете
3. ще пише	ще пишат

The Verb *To Be*

to be	*sâm*	съм

Singular

I am (not)	аз (не) съм
You are (not)	ти (не) си
He is (not)	той (не) е
She is (not)	тя (не) е
It is (not)	то (не) е

Plural

We are (not)	ние (не) сме
You are (not)	вие (не) сте
They are (not)	те (не) са

Word Order

Bulgarian word order is rather flexible. There are no strict rules as to where the parts of a sentence should stand. The adjective is about the only part of the sentence with a rigid place – always before the noun it modifies.

Questions are formed with the interrogative particle **ли** placed after the verb in the sentence:

Ходиш на кино.	Ходиш **ли** на кино?
Искат чай.	Искат **ли** чай?

Or with one of the interrogative words (as in English):

Who's calling?	**Кой** звъни?
How much is that?	**Колко** струва това?

The word order in questions in Bulgarian is very much the same as in English.

MEETING PEOPLE

ЗАПОЗНАНСТВО

WORDS TO REMEMBER	*ZAPOM'NETE*	ЗАПОМНЕТЕ
Yes.	*Da.*	Да.
No.	*Ne.*	Не.
Please.	*Ako o'bichate.*	Ако обичате.
Pardon?	*'Molya?*	Моля?
Thank you./Thanks.	*Blagoda'rya!*	Благодаря!
Excuse me.	*Izvi'nete.*	Извинете.
Sorry.	*Sâzha'lyavam.*	Съжалявам.
I don't understand!	*Ne raz'biram!*	Не разбирам!

GREETINGS	*'POZDRAVI*	ПОЗДРАВИ
Welcome!	*Dob're do'shâl/ do'shla/do'shli!*	Добре дошъл *(m)*/ дошла *(f)*/дошли *(pl)*!
Good morning!	*Dob'ro 'utro!*	Добро утро!
Good afternoon!	*'Dobâr den!*	Добър ден!
Good evening!	*'Dobâr 'vecher!*	Добър вечер!
Goodnight!	*'Leka nosht!*	Лека нощ!
Have a nice day!	*Pri'yaten den!*	Приятен ден!
Have a nice evening!	*Pri'yatna 'vecher!*	Приятна вечер!
Goodbye!	*Do'vizhdane!*	Довиждане!
See you soon!	*Do 'skoro!*	До скоро!
Bye!	*'Chao!*	Чао!

MEETING PEOPLE

Forms of Address

In Bulgarian, as in many other languages, there are two ways to address people: the informal ***mu*** *and the more formal* ***Bue****. Bulgarians use* ***Bue*** *when talking with strangers or when expressing their respectful attitude.* ***Tu*** *is reserved for more informal circumstances.*

Mr...	*Gospo'din...*	Господин...
Mrs...	*Gospo'zha...*	Госпожа...
Miss...	*Gos'pozhitsa...*	Госпожица...
Sir!	*Gospo'dine!*	Господине!
Madam!	*Gos'pozho!*	Госпожо!

Breaking the Ice	***Da rasto'pim le'da***	**Да разтопим леда**
Do you speak Bulgarian? – Yes, but not very well./A little./ Not at all.	*Go'vorite li 'bâlgarski?* *– Da, no ne 'mnogo dob're./'Malko./ 'Nikak.*	Говорите ли български? – Да, но не много добре./Малко./ Никак.
I don't speak Bulgarian.	*Ne go'vorya 'bâlgarski.*	Не говоря български.
Hello.	*Zdra'vey./ Zdra'veyte.*	Здравей *(sg)*./ Здравейте *(pl)*.
Hi.	*'Zdrasti!*	Здрасти!
I'm glad to meet you.	*Pri'yatno mi e da se zapo'znaem.*	Приятно ми е да се запознаем.

What's your name?	*Kak se 'kazvash/ 'kazvate?*	Как се казваш *(sg)*/ казвате *(pl)*?
My name is...	*'Kazvam se...*	Казвам се...
How old are you?	*Na 'kolko go'dini si/ ste?*	На колко години си *(sg)*/сте *(pl)*?
How are you? Fine. And you?	*Kak si/ste?* *Do'bre, a ti/'vie?*	Как си *(sg)*/сте *(pl)*? Добре, а ти *(sg)*/вие *(pl)*?
Let me introduce you to... my friend. my friends. my husband.	*'Neka Vi pret'stavya na...* *'moya pri'yatel.* *'moite pri'yateli.* *'moya sâ'pruk.*	Нека Ви представя на... моя приятел. моите приятели. моя съпруг.
This is... my girlfriend. my husband. my wife.	*To'va e...* *'moyata pri'yatelka.* *'moya sâ'pruk.* *'moyata sâ'pruga.*	Това е... моята приятелка. моят съпруг. моята съпруга.

Starting Conversation	*Da za'vârzhem 'razgovor*	Да завържем разговор
How was your trip?	*Kak 'mina pâ'tuvaneto vi?*	Как мина пътуването ви?
– Great./It was OK./ So-so./It was awful.	*– Chu'desno./Dob're./ 'Gore-'dolu./U'zhasno.*	– Чудесно./Добре./ Горе-долу./Ужасно.
When did you arrive in Bulgaria?	*Ko'ga pris'tignahte v Bâl'garia?*	Кога пристигнахте в България?

– A week ago/ a few days ago/ yesterday.	*– Pre'di 'sedmitsa/ pre'di 'nyakolko dni/ 'fchera.*	– Преди седмица/ преди няколко дни/ вчера.
How long will you stay in our country? – A few days/ a week/a month.	*'Kolko 'vreme shte os'tanete f stra'nata? – 'Nyakolko dni/ 'sedmitsa/'mesets.*	Колко време ще останете в страната? – Няколко дни/ седмица/месец.
Where are you staying? – At a hotel/ in a private house/ with some friends.	*Kâ'de ste ot'sednali? – F ho'tel/ f 'chasna kvar'tira/ u pri'yateli.*	Къде сте отседнали? – В хотел/ в частна квартира/ у приятели.
How do you like Bulgaria? – It's great.	*Ha'resva li vi Bâl'garia? – Da, 'mnogo.*	Харесва ли ви България? – Да, много.
Are you here on holiday? – Yes./No, on business.	*Na po'chifka li ste tuk? – Da./Ne, tuk sâm po 'rabota.*	На почивка ли сте тук? – Да./Не, тук съм по работа.

Nationalities	*Natsio'nalnosti*	Националности
Where are you from? – I come from Britain/ the USA.	*Otkâ'de ste? – As sâm ot Velikobri'tania/ Sasht, 'Shtatite.*	Откъде сте? – Аз съм от Великобритания/ САЩ, Щатите.

I'm...	*As sâm...*	Аз съм...
English.	*angli'chanin/*	англичанин *(m)*/
	angli'chanka.	англичанка *(f)*.
British.	*bri'tanets/*	британец *(m)*/
	bri'tanka.	британка *(f)*.
American.	*ameri'kanets/*	американец *(m)*/
	ameri'kanka.	американка *(f)*.

I was born in Scotland, but I live in England.	*Ro'den/a sâm f Shot'landia, no zhi'veya f 'Anglia.*	Роден *(m)*/а *(f)* съм в Шотландия, но живея в Англия.

Occupations | *Pro'fesii* | Професии

What do you do?	*Kak'vo ra'botite?*	Какво работите?

I'm a/an...	*As sâm....*	Аз съм....
actor	*ak'tyor*	актьор
actress	*ak'trisa*	актриса
artist	*hu'dozhnik*	художник *(m)*
	hu'dozhnichka	художничка *(f)*
computer programmer	*kom'pyutâren progra'mist*	компютърен програмист
cook	*got'vach*	готвач *(m)*
	got'vachka	готвачка *(f)*
doctor	*'lekar*	лекар *(m)*
	'lekarka	лекарка *(f)*
engineer	*inzhe'ner*	инженер
journalist	*zhurna'list*	журналист *(m)*
	zhurna'liska	журналистка *(f)*

lawyer	*advo'kat*	адвокат *(m)*
	advo'katka	адвокатка *(f)*
mechanic	*me'hanik*	механик
nurse	*medi'tsinska ses'tra*	медицинска сестра *(f)*
student	*stu'dent*	студент *(m)*
	stu'dentka	студентка *(f)*
teacher	*u'chitel*	учител *(m)*
	u'chitelka	учителка *(f)*
writer	*pi'satel*	писател *(m)*
	pi'satelka	писателка *(f)*
I'm a..., but I work as a...	*Po pro'fesia sâm..., no ra'botya ka'to...*	По професия съм..., но работя като...

Family | *Se'meystvo* | Семейство

Are you married?	*'Zhenen/ O'mâzhena li ste?*	Женен *(m)*/ Омъжена *(f)* ли сте?
Have you got any children?	*'Imate li de'tsa?*	Имате ли деца?
– Yes, a boy and a girl.	*– Da, mom'che i mo'miche.*	– Да, момче и момиче.
– No, I haven't.	*– Ne, 'nyamam.*	– Не, нямам.
I come from a small/ big family.	*'Moeto se'meystvo e 'malko/go'lyamo.*	Моето семейство е малко/голямо.
I have a father, mother, brother and sister.	*'Imam ba'shta, 'mayka, brat i ses'tra.*	Имам баща, майка, брат и сестра.

USEFUL WORDS AND PHRASES	PO'LEZNI 'DUMI I 'IZRAZI	ПОЛЕЗНИ ДУМИ И ИЗРАЗИ
aunt	*'lelya*	леля
cousin	*bratof'chet*	братовчед *(m)*
	bratof'chetka	братовчедка *(f)*
daughter	*dâshte'rya*	дъщеря
divorced	*raz'veden*	разведен *(m)*
	raz'vedena	разведена *(f)*
granddaughter	*'vnuchka*	внучка
grandfather	*'dyado*	дядо
grandmother	*'baba*	баба
grandson	*vnuk*	внук
husband	*sâ'pruk*	съпруг
married	*'zhenen*	женен *(m)*
	o'mâzhena	омъжена *(f)*
relative	*rod'nina*	роднина
school	*u'chilishte*	училище
single	*ne'zhenen*	неженен *(m)*
	neo'mâzhena	неомъжена *(f)*
son	*sin*	син
uncle	*'chicho*	чичо
university	*universi'tet*	университет
widow	*vdo'vitsa*	вдовица
widower	*vdo'vets*	вдовец
wife	*sâ'pruga*	съпруга

REGARDS AND COMPLIMENTS	'POZDRAVI I KOMPLI'MENTI	ПОЗДРАВИ И КОМПЛИМЕНТИ
Give my regards to...	*'Mnogo 'pozdravi na...*	Много поздрави на...

The pleasure is all mine.	*Udo'volstvieto e 'moe.*	Удоволствието е мое.
You look great.	*Iz'glezhdash prek'rasno.*	Изглеждаш прекрасно.
Fabulous dress.	*Stra'hotna 'roklya.*	Страхотна рокля.

Opinions and Preferences | *'Mnenia i pretpochi'tania* | Мнения и предпочитания

I like...	*Ha'resvam...*	Харесвам...
I love...	*O'bicham...*	Обичам...
I hate...	*'Mrazya...*	Мразя...
I prefer... to...	*Pretpo'chitam... pret...*	Предпочитам... пред...
I don't care.	*Fse mi e ed'no.*	Все ми е едно.
Do you like...?	*Ha'resva li ti/ vi...?*	Харесва ли ти *(sg)*/ ви *(pl)*...?
Yes, very much.	*Da, 'mnogo.*	Да, много.
So-so.	*'Gore-'dolu.*	Горе-долу.
No, not at all.	*Ne, 'nikak.*	Не, никак.

How do you like the...	*Kak ti se 'struva...*	Как ти се струва...
album?	*al'buma?*	албумът?
book?	*'knigata?*	книгата?
movie?	*'filma?*	филмът?
– I think it's...	*– 'Struva mi se...*	– Струва ми се...
awful.	*u'zhasen.*	ужасен.
boring.	*'skuchen.*	скучен.
great.	*stra'hoten.*	страхотен.

Body Language

Bulgarians, being a southern nation, tend to be rather temperamental and don't rely only on mere speech to express themselves. Facial expression, tone of voice, manners and gestures all play an important role in conveying their attitude. Yet, the foreigner would have no difficulty understanding locals, with one essential exception: when shaking their head from side to side, Bulgarians mean "yes", while the nodding of the head signifies "no".

TIME AND DATES

ВРЕМЕ И КАЛЕНДАР

Telling the Time

Bulgaria uses Eastern European Time, which is two hours ahead of Greenwich. Daylight Saving Time is usually between March and October.

Bulgarians normally follow the European practice of writing dates, i.e. the date comes first, then the month and, finally, the year. So 07.04.2003 will read the seventh of April, and not July the 4th, as in the USA, for instance.

TIME	*ASTRONO'MICHESKO 'VREME*	АСТРОНОМИЧЕСКО ВРЕМЕ
What time is it?	*'Kolko e cha'sa?*	Колко е часът?
– One o'clock.	*– E'din cha'sa.*	– Един часът.
One fifteen.	*E'din i pet'nayset.*	Един и петнадесет.
Half past one.	*E'din i polo'vina.*	Един и половина.

Quarter to two.	*Dva bes pet'nayset.*	Два без петнадесет.
Two o'clock.	*Dva cha'sa.*	Два часът.

Dates	***'Dati***	**Дати**
What's the date today?	*Ko'ya 'data e dnes?*	Коя дата е днес?
– Today is the first of March/ the eighth of September.	*– Dnes e 'pârvi mart/ 'osmi sep'temvri.*	– Днес е първи март/ осми септември.

Days of the Week	***'Dnite na 'sedmitsata***	**Дните на седмицата**
Monday	*pone'delnik*	понеделник
Tuesday	*'ftornik*	вторник
Wednesday	*'sryada*	сряда
Thursday	*chet'vârtâk*	четвъртък
Friday	*'petâk*	петък
Saturday	*'sâbota*	събота
Sunday	*ne'delya*	неделя

Months	***'Mesetsi***	**Месеци**
January	*yanu'ari*	януари
February	*fevru'ari*	февруари
March	*mart*	март
April	*ap'ril*	април
May	*may*	май
June	*'yuni*	юни

July	*'yuli*	юли
August	*'avgust*	август
September	*sep'temvri*	септември
October	*ok'tomvri*	октомври
November	*no'emvri*	ноември
December	*de'kemvri*	декември

Seasons / *Se'zoni* / Сезони

spring	*'prolet*	пролет
summer	*'lyato*	лято
autumn/fall	*'esen*	есен
winter	*'zima*	зима

Years / *Go'dini* / Години

year	*go'dina*	година
a hundred years ago	*pre'di sto go'dini*	преди 100 години
ten years ago	*pre'di 'deset go'dini*	преди 10 години
last year	*'minalata go'dina*	миналата година
this year	*'tazi go'dina*	тази година
next year	*dogo'dina*	догодина
in five years	*slet pet go'dini*	след 5 години
in twenty years	*slet 'dvayset go'dini*	след 20 години

Epochs / *E'pohi* / Епохи

BC	*pre'di Hris'ta*	преди Христа
AD	*slet Hris'ta*	след Христа
ancient times	*'drevnost*	древност

Middle Ages	*srednove'kovie*	средновековие
modern times	*sâ'vremie*	съвремие
century	*vek*	век
a thousand years	*hilyado'letie*	хилядолетие
era	*'era*	ера

TIME ADVERBS	*NA'RECHIA ZA 'VREME*	НАРЕЧИЯ ЗА ВРЕМЕ
the day before yesterday	*'onziden*	онзиден
yesterday	*'fchera*	вчера
last night	*'snoshti*	снощи
today	*dnes*	днес
in the morning	*sutrin'ta*	сутринта
in the afternoon	*sle'dobet*	следобед
tonight	*do'vechera*	довечера
tomorrow	*'utre*	утре
the day after tomorrow	*'vdrugiden*	вдругиден
next week	*'sledvashtata 'sedmitsa*	следващата седмица
next month	*'sledvashtia 'mesets*	следващия месец
past	*'minalo*	минало
present	*nasto'yashte*	настояще
future	*'bâdeshte*	бъдеще
always	*'vinagi*	винаги
never	*'nikoga*	никога
often	*'chesto*	често
rarely	*'ryatko*	рядко
usually	*obikno'veno*	обикновено
sometimes	*po'nyakoga*	понякога
fortnight	*dve 'sedmitsi*	две седмици

WEATHER

КЛИМАТ

What's the weather like today?	*Kak'vo e 'vremeto dnes?*	Какво е времето днес?
– It's...		
cloudy.	*– 'Oblachno e.*	– Облачно е.
cold.	*Stu'deno e.*	Студено е.
foggy.	*Mâg'livo e.*	Мъгливо е.
hot.	*Go'reshto e.*	Горещо е.
rainy.	*Dâzh'dovno e.*	Дъждовно е.
sunny.	*'Slânchevo e.*	Слънчево е.
warm.	*'Toplo e.*	Топло е.
windy.	*Vetro'vito e.*	Ветровито е.
What will be the weather like tomorrow?	*Kak'vo shte 'bâde 'vremeto 'utre?*	Какво ще бъде времето утре?
– It will...	*– Shte...*	– Ще...
be wet.	*'bâde 'vlazhno.*	бъде влажно.
rain.	*va'li dâsht.*	вали дъжд.
snow.	*va'li snyak.*	вали сняг.

NUMBERS AND MEASURES

ЧИСЛА И МЕРКИ

CARDINAL NUMBERS	*CHIS'LITELNI 'BROYNI*	ЧИСЛИТЕЛНИ БРОЙНИ
zero	*'nula*	нула
one	*e'din*	един *(m)*
	ed'na	една *(f)*
	ed'no	едно *(n)*
two	*dva*	два *(m)*
	dve	две *(f, n)*
three	*tri*	три
four	*'chetiri*	четири
five	*pet*	пет
six	*shest*	шест
seven	*'sedem*	седем
eight	*'osem*	осем
nine	*'devet*	девет
ten	*'deset*	десет
eleven	*edi'nayset*	единадесет
twelve	*dva'nayset*	дванадесет
thirteen	*tri'nayset*	тринадесет
fourteen	*chetiri'nayset*	четиринадесет

fifteen	*pet'nayset*	петнадесет
sixteen	*shes'nayset*	шестнадесет
seventeen	*sedem'nayset*	седемнадесет
eighteen	*osem'nayset*	осемнадесет
nineteen	*devet'nayset*	деветнадесет
twenty	*'dvayset*	двадесет
twenty-one	*'dvayset i ed'no*	двадесет и едно
twenty-two	*'dvayset i dve*	двадесет и две
thirty	*'triyset*	тридесет
forty	*che'tiriyset*	четиридесет
fifty	*pede'set*	петдесет
sixty	*shey'set*	шестдесет
seventy	*sedemde'set*	седемдесет
eighty	*osemde'set*	осемдесет
ninety	*devede'set*	деветдесет
a hundred	*sto*	сто
a hundred and one	*sto i ed'no*	сто и едно
a hundred and two	*sto i dve*	сто и две
two hundred	*'dvesta*	двеста
three hundred	*'trista*	триста
four hundred	*'chetiristotin*	четиристотин
five hundred	*'petstotin*	петстотин
six hundred	*'shestotin*	шестстотин
seven hundred	*'sedemstotin*	седемстотин
eight hundred	*'osemstotin*	осемстотин
nine hundred	*'devet-stotin*	деветстотин
a thousand	*hi'lyada*	хиляда
two thousand	*dve 'hilyadi*	две хиляди
a million	*mili'on*	милион
billion	*mili'art*	милиард

Ordinal Numbers	*Chis'litelni 'redni*	Числителни редни
first	*'pârvi*	първи
second	*'ftori*	втори
third	*'treti*	трети
fourth	*chet'vârti*	четвърти
fifth	*'peti*	пети
sixth	*'shesti*	шести
seventh	*'sedmi*	седми
eighth	*'osmi*	осми
ninth	*de'veti*	девети
tenth	*de'seti*	десети
eleventh	*edi'nayseti*	единадесети
twelfth	*dva'nayseti*	дванадесети
thirteenth	*tri'nayseti*	тринадесети
fourteenth	*chetiri'nayseti*	четиринадесети
fifteenth	*pet'nayseti*	петнадесети
sixteenth	*shes'nayseti*	шестнадесети
seventeenth	*sedem'nayseti*	седемнадесети
eighteenth	*osem'nayseti*	осемнадесети
nineteenth	*devet'nayseti*	деветнадесети
twentieth	*'dvayseti*	двадесети
twenty-first	*'dvayset i 'pârvi*	двадесет и първи
twenty-second	*'dvayset i 'ftori*	двадесет и втори
thirtieth	*'triyseti*	тридесети
fortieth	*che'tiriyseti*	четиридесети
fiftieth	*pede'seti*	петдесети
sixtieth	*shey'seti*	шестдесети
seventieth	*sedemde'seti*	седемдесети
eightieth	*osemde'seti*	осемдесети
ninetieth	*devede'seti*	деветдесети
hundredth	*'stoten*	стотен

MEASURES	*'MERKI*	МЕРКИ
gram	*gram*	грам
quarter	*'chetvârt (250 g)*	четвърт (250 г)
kilogram	*kilo'gram*	килограм
tonne	*ton*	тон
millimetre	*mili'metâr*	милиметър
centimetre	*santi'metâr*	сантиметър
metre	*'metâr*	метър
kilometre	*kilo'metâr*	километър
litre	*'litâr*	литър
height	*visochi'na*	височина
width	*shiri'na*	ширина
length	*dâlzhi'na*	дължина
depth	*dâlbochi'na*	дълбочина
square centimetre	*kvad'raten santi'metâr*	квадратен сантиметър
square metre	*kvad'raten 'metâr*	квадратен метър
cubic metre	*ku'bicheski 'metâr*	кубически метър

MONEY AND BANKS

ПАРИ И БАНКИ

The national currency of Bulgaria is the Bulgarian Lev. 1 Lev amounts to 100 stotinki. In the wake of the devaluation, shaking the Bulgarian financial system in 1996, Bulgaria's lev has been managed by an IMF-appointed Currency Board, which pegged it to the German Mark at the rate of 1 BGL = DM 1. With the entry of the unified European currency, 1 Euro equals to 1.955 BGL. The exchange rate of the dollar varies from day to day at the approximate rate of US $ 1 = 2 BGL. It's always best to check with a bank, exchange bureaux, or at the reception in your hotel about the exchange rate for the day. The opening hours for banks are 9 am – 4 pm from Monday to Friday, while exchange bureaux are usually open until 6 pm, some even working round the clock.

Is there a bank near here?	*'Ima li nab'lizo 'banka?*	Има ли наблизо банка?
Where can I change some money?	*Kâ'de 'moga da obme'nya pa'ri?*	Къде мога да обменя пари?

How many leva can I get for 50 pounds?	*'Kolko 'leva shte po'lucha za pede'set 'liri?*	Колко лева ще получа за 50 лири?
What's the exchange rate for today?	*Ka'kâf e ob'menia kurs za de'nya?*	Какъв е обменният курс за деня?
Do you take credit cards?	*Pri'emate li 'kreditni 'karti?*	Приемате ли кредитни карти?
Could you cash this traveller's cheque/ Eurocheque?	*'Mozhete li da osreb'rite 'tozi 'pâtnicheski chek/ 'Evrochek?*	Можете ли да осребрите този пътнически чек/ Еврочек?
I'd like to open a bank account.	*'Iskam da si ot'kria 'bankova 'smetka.*	Искам да си открия банкова сметка.
Here's my bank account number.	*'Eto 'nomera na 'moyata 'bankova 'smetka.*	Ето номера на моята банкова сметка.

Useful Words and Phrases | *Po'lezni 'dumi i 'izrazi* | Полезни думи и изрази

ATM	*banko'mat*	банкомат
currency	*va'luta*	валута
dollar	*'dolar*	долар
Euro	*'evro*	евро
exchange rate	*ob'menen kurs*	обменен курс
GB pound	*bri'tanska 'lira*	британска лира
receipt	*'raspiska*	разписка

TRAVELLING

ПЪТУВАНЕ

CUSTOMS	*'MITNITSA*	МИТНИЦА
Passport control.	*Pas'porten kon'trol.*	Паспортен контрол.
Your passport, please.	*Pas'porta, 'molya.*	Паспорта, моля.
Reason for travel?	*Tsel na pâ'tuvaneto?*	Цел на пътуването?
Are you a tourist?	*Tu'rist li ste?*	Турист ли сте?
Yes./No, I'm here on business.	*Da./Ne, tuk sâm po 'rabota.*	Да./Не, тук съм по работа.
How long will you stay?	*'Kolko 'vreme shte os'tanete?*	Колко време ще останете?
A few days/two weeks/a month.	*'Nyakolko dni/dve 'sedmitsi/'mesets.*	Няколко дни/две седмици/месец.
Have you got something to declare?	*'Imate li 'neshto za dekla'rirane?*	Имате ли нещо за деклариране?

No./Yes, two bottles of alcohol and two cartons of cigarettes.	*Ne./Da, dve bu'tilki alko'hol i dva 'steka tsi'gari.*	Не./Да, две бутилки алкохол и два стека цигари.
Open the suitcase, please!	*Otvo'rete 'kufara, 'molya!*	Отворете куфара, моля!
Have a nice time in Bulgaria!	*Pri'yatno prebi'vavane v Bâl'garia!*	Приятно пребиваване в България!

Useful Words and Phrases / *Po'lezni 'dumi i 'izrazi* / Полезни думи и изрази

address	*a'dres*	адрес
alcohol	*'spirtni na'pitki*	спиртни напитки
application form	*formu'lyar*	формуляр
baggage/luggage	*ba'gash*	багаж
boot/trunk	*ba'gazhnik*	багажник
carry-on luggage	*'râchen ba'gash*	ръчен багаж
cigarettes	*tsi'gari*	цигари
date of birth	*'data na 'razhdane*	дата на раждане
driving-licence	*sho'fyorska 'knishka*	шофьорска книжка
EC-citizens	*'grazhdani na Evro'peyskia Sâ'yus*	граждани на Европейския съюз
marital status	*se'meyno polo'zhenie*	семейно положение
nationality	*natsio'nalnost*	националност
passport number	*'nomer na pas'porta*	номер на паспорта
place of birth	*'myasto na 'razhdane*	място на раждане
visa	*'viza*	виза

Travelling by Car

In Bulgaria, you drive on the right and overtake on the left. One mile is equal to 1.6 km. Speed limit on highways is 120 km/h (74 mph), in built-up areas – 50 km/h (31 mph), if not otherwise indicated. You can find a petrol station every 30 or so kilometres along the highways. You shouldn't have problems reading the road signs, as they are identical with the ones used in the other countries. Alcohol limit, when driving, equals to 1 beer, a glass of wine or 50 g alcohol. Nevertheless, you'd better refrain from drinking before driving!

RENT-A-CAR	*KO'LA POD 'NAEM*	КОЛА ПОД НАЕМ
I'd like to rent a car for...	*Bih 'iskal da na'ema ko'la za...*	Бих искал да наема кола за...
a day.	*e'din den.*	един ден.
the weekend.	*u'ikenda.*	уикенда.
a week.	*ed'na 'sedmitsa.*	една седмица.
How much is it per day?	*'Kolko 'struva na den?*	Колко струва на ден?
Is mileage/ insurance included?	*Kilomet'razha 'fklyuchen/ zastra'hofkata 'fklyuchena li e?*	Километражът включен/ застраховката включена ли е?
Should I pay a deposit?	*'Tryabva li da pla'tya de'pozit?*	Трябва ли да платя депозит?

Have you got a driving-licence?	*'Imate li sho'fyorska 'knishka?*	Имате ли шофьорска книжка?
Where can I return the car?	*Kâ'de 'moga da 'vârna ko'lata?*	Къде мога да върна колата?

At the Petrol Station	*Na benzino'stantsiata*	На бензиностанцията
Where's the nearest/ next petrol station?	*Kâ'de e 'nay-'bliskata/ 'sledvashtata benzino'stantsia?*	Къде е най-близката/ следващата бензиностанция?
Fill up the tank, please.	*Napâl'nete rezervo'ara, 'molya.*	Напълнете резервоара, моля.
I'd like... litres.	*Bih 'iskal... 'litra.*	Бих искал... литра.

Car Problems	*Prob'lemi s ko'lata*	Проблеми с колата
Is there a car repair shop near here?	*'Ima li nab'lizo 'aftoser'vis?*	Има ли наблизо автосервиз?
Please check the... oil. tyre pressure. water.	*'Molya, prove'rete... mas'loto. 'gumite. vo'data.*	Моля, проверете... маслото. гумите. водата.

I need a mechanic.	*'Tryabva mi mon'tyor.*	Трябва ми монтьор.
There's something wrong with the engine.	*'Neshto ne e na'ret s dvi'gatelya.*	Нещо не е наред с двигателя.
The car has broken down.	*Ko'lata se razva'li.*	Колата се развали.
The engine's overheating.	*Dvi'gatelya preg'ryava.*	Двигателят прегрява.
The battery's flat.	*Akumu'latora e 'padnal.*	Акумулаторът е паднал.
I need a new tyre.	*Nuzh'daya se ot 'nova 'guma.*	Нуждая се от нова гума.

Useful Words and Phrases | *Po'lezni 'dumi i 'izrazi* | Полезни думи и изрази

accident	*kata'strofa*	катастрофа
antifreeze	*anti'fris*	антифриз
battery	*akumu'lator*	акумулатор
brakes	*spi'rachki*	спирачки
car park	*'parkink*	паркинг
car wash	*'afto'mifka*	автомивка
crossroad	*krâs'tovishte*	кръстовище
diesel oil	*'dizelovo go'rivo*	дизелово гориво
distilled water	*desti'lirana vo'da*	дестилирана вода
driver's license	*sho'fyorska 'knishka*	шофьорска книжка
fine	*'globa*	глоба

gasoline	*gas*	газ
headlights	*'farove*	фарове
keys	*'klyuchove*	ключове
leaded/unleaded petrol	*o'loven/bezo'loven ben'zin*	оловен/безоловен бензин
oil	*mas'lo*	масло
puncture	*'spukana 'guma*	спукана гума
radiator	*radi'ator*	радиатор
road patrol	*'pâten poli'tseyski pat'rul*	пътен полицейски патрул
seatbelt	*pret'pazen ko'lan*	предпазен колан
spare parts	*re'zervni 'chasti*	резервни части
spark plug	*svesht*	свещ
speed limit	*ograni'chenie na skoros'ta*	ограничение на скоростта
traffic jam	*zad'râstvane*	задръстване
traffic lights	*sveto'far*	светофар
Traffic Police	*kat/'pâtna po'litsia*	КАТ/пътна полиция
trunk	*ba'gazhnik*	багажник
turn	*za'voy*	завой
tyre	*'guma*	гума
wheel	*vo'lan*	волан

RAIL TRAVEL	*PÂ'TUVANE S VLAK*	ПЪТУВАНЕ С ВЛАК
When does the train to... leave?	*Ko'ga 'trâgva 'vlaka za...?*	Кога тръгва влакът за...?
When does the train from.... arrive?	*Ko'ga pris'tiga 'vlaka ot...?*	Кога пристига влакът от...?

Is there any delay?	*'Ima li zakâs'nenie?*	Има ли закъснение?
I'd like one first-/ second-class ticket for smokers/ non-smokers for the express train to Varna.	*'Iskam e'din bi'let 'pârva/'ftora 'klasa, pu'shachi/ nepu'shachi za eks'presa za 'Varna.*	Искам един билет първа/втора класа, пушачи/ непушачи за експреса за Варна.
When's the first/ next/ last train to...?	*Ko'ga e 'pârvia/ 'sledvashtia/ pos'lednia vlak za...?*	Кога е първият/ следващият/ последният влак за...?
How much is the ticket?	*'Kolko 'struva bi'leta?*	Колко струва билетът?
Does the train stop in...?	*'Spira li 'vlaka v...?*	Спира ли влакът в...?
A single/ return ticket to Sofia.	*E'din bi'let/bi'let o'tivane i 'vrâshtane do 'Sofia.*	Един билет/билет отиване и връщане до София.
What platform does the train leave from?	*Ot koy pe'ron 'trâgva 'vlaka?*	От кой перон тръгва влакът?
Is the seat free?	*Svo'bodno li e 'myastoto?*	Свободно ли е мястото?
– Yes./No, it's taken.	*– Da./Ne, za'eto e.*	– Да./Не, заето е.
Which is this station?	*Ko'ya e 'tazi 'gara?*	Коя е тази гара?
Is there a buffet-car on this train?	*'Ima li va'gon-resto'rant vâv 'vlaka?*	Има ли вагон-ресторант във влака?

Air Travel	*Pâ'tuvane sâs samo'let*	Пътуване със самолет
How can I get to the airport?	*Kak da 'stigna do le'tishteto?*	Как да стигна до летището?
What time should I be at the airport?	*Ko'ga 'tryabva da sâm na le'tishteto?*	Кога трябва да съм на летището?
How much is the ticket?	*'Kolko 'struva bi'leta?*	Колко струва билетът?
I'd like a window seat, please.	*Bih 'iskal/ 'iskala 'myasto do pro'zoretsa.*	Бих искал *(m)*/ искала *(f)* място до прозореца.
Which is the gate for the flight to...?	*Koy 'is-hot e za samo'leta za...?*	Кой изход е за самолета за...?
I have only carry-on luggage.	*'Imam 'samo 'râchen ba'gash.*	Имам само ръчен багаж.

Boat	*Pâ'tuvane po mo're*	Пътуване по море
I'd like a ticket to...	*'Iskam e'din bi'let do...*	Искам един билет до...
When does the boat to... leave?	*Ko'ga 'trâgva 'korapcheto za...?*	Кога тръгва корабчето за...?
How long does the cruise to... take?	*'Kolko 'vreme 'trae pâ'tuvaneto do...?*	Колко време трае пътуването до...?

Taxi	***Tak'si***	**Такси**
Is there a taxi rank nearby?	*'Ima li nab'lizo sto'yanka za tak'si?*	Има ли наблизо стоянка за такси?
Could you call a taxi for me?	*'Bihte li mi po'vikali tak'si?*	Бихте ли ми повикали такси?
To the airport/ railway station/city centre, please.	*Kâm le'tishteto/ 'garata/'tsentâra, 'molya.*	Към летището/ гарата/центъра, моля.
Stop here.	*'Sprete tuk.*	Спрете тук.
Wait, please.	*Is'chakayte, 'molya.*	Изчакайте, моля.
Could you help me with the luggage?	*'Mozhe li da mi po'mognete s ba'gazha?*	Може ли да ми помогнете с багажа?
How much do I owe you?	*'Kolko vi dâl'zha?*	Колко ви дължа?

Public Transport	***Op'shtestven trans'port***	**Обществен транспорт**
Where's the bus stop?	*Kâ'de e afto'busnata 'spirka?*	Къде е автобусната спирка?
Where's the nearest underground station?	*Kâ'de e 'nay-'bliskata 'stantsia na met'roto?*	Къде е най-близката станция на метрото?
What bus should I take to the city centre?	*Koy afto'bus 'tryabva da 'vzema za 'tsentâra?*	Кой автобус трябва да взема за центъра?

Does this bus go to...?	*'Tozi afto'bus o'tiva li do...?*	Този автобус отива ли до...?
Could you tell me where I should get off?	*'Bihte li mi 'kazali kâ'de da 'slyaza?*	Бихте ли ми казали къде да сляза?
I'd like to get to...	*'Iskam da 'ida do...*	Искам да ида до...

Useful Words and Phrases — *Po'lezni 'dumi i 'izrazi* — Полезни думи и изрази

Useful Words and Phrases	*Po'lezni 'dumi i 'izrazi*	Полезни думи и изрази
a child's fare	*'detski bi'let*	детски билет
a pensioner's fare	*pensio'nerski bi'let*	пенсионерски билет
a student's fare	*stu'denski bi'let*	студентски билет
arrival	*pris'tigane*	пристигане
Bulgarian State Railways	*be-de-zhe*	БДЖ
conductor	*kon'duktor*	кондуктор
departure	*zami'navane*	заминаване
express (train)	*eks'pres*	експрес
fast train	*bârs vlak*	бърз влак
luggage	*ba'gash*	багаж
non-smokers	*nepu'shachi*	непушачи
railway booking office	*byu'ro za predva'ritelna pro'dazhba na bi'leti*	бюро за предварителна продажба на билети
railway station	*('zhe'pe) 'gara*	(ЖП) гара
sleeper/sleeping-car	*'spalen va'gon*	спален вагон
slow train	*'pâtnicheski vlak*	пътнически влак
smokers	*pu'shachi*	пушачи
ticket	*bi'let*	билет
ticket desk	*gi'she za bi'leti*	гише за билети
timetable	*raspi'sanie*	разписание

ACCOMMODATION

НАСТАНЯВАНЕ

Every year Bulgaria sees the opening of a great number of new private-owned accommodations and, accordingly, a better quality of service. One can choose between 3-, 4-, and 5-star hotels. However, if travelling on a budget, you can always check with the accommodation bureax to find private rooms or hostels. Except in big ski and coastal resorts, reservation is rarely necessary.

Accommodation	*Nasta'nyavane*	Настаняване
Accommodation Bureau	*Kvar'tirno byu'ro*	Квартирно бюро
Hostel	*Turis'ticheska 'spalnya*	Туристическа спалня
Hotel	*Ho'tel*	Хотел
Private Rooms	*'Chasna kvar'tira*	Частна квартира
Rest Home	*Po'chivna 'stantsia*	Почивна станция

Accommodation

At the Hotel | *F ho'tela* | В хотела

Checking In	*Regi'stratsia*	Регистрация
Good day./Good evening.	*'Dobâr den./'Dobâr 'vecher.*	Добър ден./Добър вечер.
Do you have any rooms available?	*'Imate li svo'bodni 'stai?*	Имате ли свободни стаи?
Yes./No, it's full.	*Da./Ne, 'fsichko e za'eto.*	Да./Не, всичко е заето.
I have a reservation.	*'Imam rezer'vatsia.*	Имам резервация.
My name is...	*'Imeto mi e...*	Името ми е...
I'd like a single/double room with a bathroom for... days.	*'Iskam edi'nichna/'dvoyna 'staya s 'banya za... dni.*	Искам единична/двойна стая с баня за... дни.
My room number is...	*'Nomera na 'stayata mi e...*	Номерът на стаята ми е...
I'm leaving tomorrow.	*Na'puskam 'utre.*	Напускам утре.
The bill, please.	*'Smetkata, 'molya.*	Сметката, моля.
I'll pay in cash.	*Shte pla'tya v broy.*	Ще платя в брой.

You May Hear

Your passport, please.	*Pas'porta, 'molya.*
Fill in this form, please.	*'Molya, popâl'nete 'tozi formu'lyar.*
Sign here.	*Potpi'shete tuk.*

Requests	Za'pitvania	Запитвания
Does the hotel have a garage?	*'Ima li ho'tela ga'rash?*	Има ли хотелът гараж?
Do you change money here?	*Ob'menyate li pa'ri tuk?*	Обменяте ли пари тук?
Is there a satellite/ cable TV in the room?	*'Ima li sate'lit/ 'kabelna tele'vizia f 'stayata?*	Има ли сателит/ кабелна телевизия в стаята?
Is breakfast included?	*'Fklyuchena li e za'kuska?*	Включена ли е закуска?
How much is the room per day?	*'Kolko 'struva 'stayata na den?*	Колко струва стаята на ден?
Do you take credit cards?	*Pri'emate li 'kreditni 'karti?*	Приемате ли кредитни карти?
Would you wake me up at... o'clock?	*Shte me sâ'budite li v... cha'sa?*	Ще ме събудите ли в... часа?

When's breakfast, lunch, dinner?	*F 'kolko cha'sa e za'kuskata, o'byada, ve'cheryata?*	В колко часа е закуската, обядът, вечерята?
Do you have a safe?	*'Imate li seyf?*	Имате ли сейф?
Would you bring a bottle of mineral water, some coffee and breakfast to my room?	*'Bihte li mi do'nesli bu'tilka mine'ralna vo'da, ka'fe i za'kuska f 'stayata?*	Бихте ли ми донесли бутилка минерална вода, кафе и закуска в стаята?
Is there any message for me?	*'Ima li sâop'shtenie za men?*	Има ли съобщение за мен?
When should I vacate the room?	*Ko'ga 'tryabva da osvobo'dya 'stayata?*	Кога трябва да освободя стаята?
Could you call a taxi for me?	*'Mozhete li da mi po'vikate tak'si?*	Можете ли да ми повикате такси?

Complaints — *Op'lakvania* — Оплаквания

In the bathroom there's no...	*V 'banyata 'nyama...*	В банята няма...
soap.	*sa'pun.*	сапун.
toilet paper.	*toa'letna har'tia.*	тоалетна хартия.
towel.	*hav'lia.*	хавлия.

The room hasn't been cleaned.	*'Stayata ne e po'chistena.*	Стаята не е почистена.
The window won't open.	*Pro'zoretsa ne se ot'varya.*	Прозорецът не се отваря.
The TV/shower is not working.	*Tele'vizora/'dusha ne ra'boti.*	Телевизорът/душът не работи.
There isn't any hot water.	*'Nyama 'topla vo'da.*	Няма топла вода.

Useful Words and Phrases / *Po'lezni 'dumi i 'izrazi* / Полезни думи и изрази

air-conditioner	*klima'tik*	климатик
balcony	*bal'kon*	балкон
bathroom	*'banya*	баня
bed	*leg'lo*	легло
bed and breakfast	*leg'lo i za'kuska*	легло и закуска
blanket	*ode'yalo*	одеяло
breakfast	*za'kuska*	закуска
dinner	*ve'cherya*	вечеря
emergency exit	*ava'rien 'is-hot*	авариен изход
fire escape	*'is-hot pri po'zhar*	изход при пожар
key	*'klyuch*	ключ
lift	*asan'syor*	асансьор
lounge	*foa'ye*	фоайе
lunch	*'obet*	обед
maid	*kameri'erka*	камериерка
manager	*up'ravitel*	управител

mini-bar	*'minibar*	минибар
pillow	*vâz'glavnitsa*	възглавница
pull	*drâp'ni*	дръпни
push	*but'ni*	бутни
receptionist	*admini'strator/ admini'stratorka*	администратор *(m)*/ администраторка *(f)*
restaurant	*resto'rant*	ресторант
room	*'staya*	стая
room service	*'rumsârvis*	румсървис
shower	*dush*	душ
sink	*'mifka*	мивка
toilet	*toa'letna*	тоалетна
TV set	*tele'vizor*	телевизор

Renting an Apartment/ a Villa — *Aparta'ment/ 'vila pod 'naem* — Апартамент/ вила под наем

I'd like to rent an apartment/a villa for... days.	*'Iskam da na'ema aparta'ment/'vila za... dni.*	Искам да наема апартамент/вила за... дни.
Should I pay a deposit?	*'Tryabva li da vne'sa de'pozit?*	Трябва ли да внеса депозит?
When does the maid come?	*Ko'ga 'idva chis'tachkata?*	Кога идва чистачката?
Is kitchenware, bed linen included in the rent?	*'Fklyucheni li sa f 'naema po'sudata, 'spalnoto be'lyo?*	Включени ли са в наема посудата, спалното бельо?

Is water, electricity, heating included in the rent?	*F 'naema 'fklyucheni li sa 'ras-hodite za vo'da, osvet'lenie, otop'lenie?*	В наема включени ли са разходите за вода, осветление, отопление?
How do you start the water-heater?	*Kak se 'fklyuchva 'boylera?*	Как се включва бойлерът?
There's no water/ heating/electricity.	*'Nyama vo'da/ 'parno/tok.*	Няма вода/ парно/ток.
The shower's not working.	*'Dusha ne ra'boti.*	Душът не работи.
Where's...?	*Kâ'de e...?*	Къде е...?
Thanks for everything!	*Blagoda'rya za 'fsichko!*	Благодаря за всичко!

Useful Words and Phrases / *Po'lezni 'dumi i 'izrazi* / Полезни думи и изрази

bathroom	*'banya*	баня
bed linen	*'spalno be'lyo*	спално бельо
boiler	*'boyler*	бойлер
cooker	*got'varska 'pechka*	готварска печка
deposit	*de'pozit*	депозит
dining-room	*trape'zaria*	трапезария
electricity	*elek'trichestvo/tok*	електричество/ток
fridge	*hla'dilnik*	хладилник
heating	*'parno*	парно

iron	*yu'tia*	ютия
ironing-board	*dâs'ka za 'gladene*	дъска за гладене
kitchen	*'kuhnya*	кухня
kitchenware	*'kuhnenski 'pribori*	кухненски прибори
leak	*tech*	теч
living-room	*fseki'dnevna*	всекидневна
pillow	*vâz'glavnitsa*	възглавница
sheets	*char'shafi*	чаршафи
sink	*'mifka*	мивка
tap	*kran na chesh'ma*	кран на чешма
toilet	*toa'letna*	тоалетна
towel	*hav'lia*	хавлия
washing machine	*pe'ralnya*	пералня
water	*vo'da*	вода
water-heater	*nagre'vatel*	нагревател

FOOD

ХРАНА

Bulgaria offers a wide diversity of food, both local and foreign. Its crossroad position is reflected in the national cuisine, which combines the best of the Balkan and Oriental style of cooking. A great number of the traditional Bulgarian meals are basically vegetarian and can be a real delight for people looking for meat-free food. Since the country is home to the world-famous Bulgarian yogurt, don't leave before having tasted it!

AT THE RESTAURANT	*F RESTO'RANTA*	В РЕСТОРАНТА
A table for one/ two/three, please.	*'Masa za e'din/ 'dvama/'trima, 'molya.*	Маса за един/ двама/трима, моля.
The menu, please.	*Me'nyuto, 'molya.*	Менюто, моля.
Can I see the wine list?	*'Mozhe li da 'vidya 'listata s vi'nata?*	Може ли да видя листата с вината?

What's today's special?	*Ka'kâf e spetsiali'teta na de'nya?*	Какъв е специалитетът на деня?
Do you have vegetarian meals?	*'Imate li vegetari'anski 'yastia?*	Имате ли вегетариански ястия?
I'm vegetarian.	*As sâm vegetari'anets/ vegetari'anka.*	Аз съм вегетарианец *(m)*/ вегетарианка *(f)*.
What would you recommend?	*Kak'vo shte prepo'râchate?*	Какво ще препоръчате?
What's in this dish?	*Kak'vo sâ'dârzha to'va 'yastie?*	Какво съдържа това ястие?
I'll have...	*Za men...*	За мен...
Enjoy your meal!	*Pri'yatno 'yadene!*	Приятно ядене!
I'm allergic to...	*'Imam a'lergia kâm...*	Имам алергия към...
I'd like to try some local wine.	*Bih 'iskal/ 'iskala da o'pitam 'nyakakvo 'mesno 'vino.*	Бих искал *(m)*/ искала *(f)* да опитам някакво местно вино.
Cheers!	*Na'zdrave!*	Наздраве!
Do you have a children's menu?	*'Ima li 'detsko me'nyu?*	Има ли детско меню?
Waiter!	*Servi'tyor!*	Сервитьор!

We didn't order this!	*Ne sme po'râchvali to'va!*	Не сме поръчвали това!
Did you enjoy the meal?	*Ha'resa li vi 'yadeneto?*	Хареса ли ви яденето?
Yes, it was delicious.	*Da, 'beshe 'fkusno.*	Да, беше вкусно.
The same again, please.	*'Oshte ved'nâsh ot 'sâshtoto, 'molya.*	Още веднъж от същото, моля.
I've had enough, thank you.	*'Yadoh dos'tatâchno, blagoda'rya.*	Ядох достатъчно, благодаря.
The bill, please.	*'Smetkata, 'molya.*	Сметката, моля.
Service is included in the bill.	*Ser'viza e 'fklyuchen f 'smetkata.*	Сервизът е включен в сметката.

Useful Words and Phrases / *Po'lezni 'dumi i 'izrazi* / Полезни думи и изрази

ashtray	*pepel'nik*	пепелник
bill	*'smetka*	сметка
bottle	*bu'tilka*	бутилка
chair	*stol*	стол
corkscrew	*tirbu'shon*	тирбушон
cup	*'chasha*	чаша
fork	*'vilitsa*	вилица
glass	*'stâklena 'chasha*	стъклена чаша
knife	*nosh*	нож
menu	*me'nyu*	меню
napkin	*sal'fetka*	салфетка

plate	*chi'nia*	чиния
service	*op'sluzhvane*	обслужване
table	*'masa*	маса
tablespoon	*'supena lâ'zhitsa*	супена лъжица
teaspoon	*'chaena lâ'zhichka*	чаена лъжичка
tip	*bak'shish*	бакшиш
today's special	*spetsiali'tet na de'nya*	специалитет на деня
toothpick	*'klechka za 'zâbi*	клечка за зъби
vegetarian meal	*vegetari'ansko 'yastie*	вегетарианско ястие
waiter	*servi'tyor*	сервитьор
wine list	*'lista s vi'na*	листа с вина
wineglass	*'vinena 'chasha*	винена чаша

Spices and Condiments	*Pot'prafki*	Подправки
black pepper	*'cheren pi'per*	черен пипер
butter	*mas'lo*	масло
cinnamon	*ka'nela*	канела
cream	*sme'tana*	сметана
fennel	*'kopâr*	копър
garlic	*'chesân*	чесън
hot peppers	*'lyuti 'chushki*	люти чушки
margarine	*marga'rin*	маргарин
mayonnaise	*mayo'neza*	майонеза
mustard	*gor'chitsa*	горчица
oil	*'olio*	олио
olive oil	*zeh'tin*	зехтин
onion	*luk*	лук
parsley	*magda'nos*	магданоз
salt	*sol*	сол
sugar	*'zahar*	захар
vinegar	*o'tset*	оцет

A look at ploshtad Narodno Sâbranie and the domes of Alexandâr Nevski Cathedral, Sofia

People's Theatre Ivan Vazov, Sofia

▲ The Roman Theatre (4th century AD), Plovdiv

◄ The Old Quarter, Plovdiv

Tsarevets medieval fortress at night, Veliko Târnovo

The coastal town of Balchik

The Black Sea resorts provide ample opportunities for relaxation

© Chavdar Naydenov

The picturesque Bâbrek lake in the Rila Mountain

© Nikola Laoutliev

Autumn in Bulgarian mountains

▲ The Church of Sveta Bogoroditsa, Plovdiv

◄ Dryanovski Monastery near Veliko Târnovo

Roman remains, Hisarya

Etâra, near Gabrovo, boasts some of the finest examples of Revival architecture

Bulgarian winter tale

Menu Highlights

SALADS

Шопска *('Shopska)* – chopped cucumbers, tomatoes and green peppers, spiced with oil and finely chopped onion, and topped with grated cheese.

Селска *('Selska)* – chopped cucumbers, tomatoes and roasted peppers, spiced with oil and topped with crumbled cheese and finely chopped parsley.

Овчарска *(Of'charska)* – There are some regional varieties but it basically includes chopped cucumbers and tomatoes, roasted peppers, yellow cheese, ham, mushrooms and sweet corn, topped with cheese, slices of hard-boiled egg and some olives.

Млечна *('Mlechna)* – Also known as *Snezhanka* or *Trakiyska*, this salad is a delicious mixture of yogurt and finely chopped cucumbers, spiced with garlic and dill, and topped with crushed walnuts.

Руска *('Ruska)* – boiled potatoes, green peas, carrots, pickles, chopped sausage, hard-boiled eggs, all mixed in mayonnaise.

Зелена/Великденска *(Ze'lena/Ve'likdenska)* – Traditionally served in spring, this salad is made of finely shredded lettuce, spiced with oil and topped with olives and boiled eggs.

Зелева *('Zeleva)* – made of finely shredded cabbage and grated carrots, spiced with oil and vinegar.

Кьопоолу *('Kyopoolu)* – spicy salad made of baked eggplant and peppers, spiced with salt, oil and vinegar, and topped with crushed walnuts.

Menu Highlights

SOUPS

Шкембе чорба *(Shkem'be chor'ba)* – boiled tripe spiced with black pepper and garlic, served with vinegar and hot peppers.

Таратор *(Tara'tor)* – This refreshing summer dish is made of chopped cucumbers mixed with shaken yogurt and crushed walnuts, and spiced with salt, oil, dill and garlic.

STARTERS

Чушка бюрек *('Chushka byu'rek)* – roasted peppers stuffed with a mixture of eggs, crumbled cheese, finely chopped parsley and black pepper, then breaded and fried.

Кашкавал пане *(Kashka'val pa'ne)* – yellow cheese coated in breadcrumbs and fried.

Сирене по шопски *('Sirene po 'shopski)* – white cheese, mushrooms, olives, tomato sauce and egg, baked in a clay pot.

Сирене по тракийски *('Sirene po tra'kiyski)* – as *Sirene po shopski*, but with added meat or sausage.

Лозови сарми *('Lozovi sar'mi)* – vine leaves stuffed with a mixture of rice, finely chopped onion, minced meat, mint and pepper, then boiled. Usually served with yogurt.

Пържени тиквички *('Pârzheni 'tikvichki)* – fried slices of zucchini served with yogurt and garlic.

Миш-маш *(Mish-mash)* – eggs scrambled with cheese, diced peppers and grated tomatoes.

Menu Highlights

MEALS

Гювеч *(Gyu'vech)* – The vegetarian variety includes diced potatoes, tomatoes, eggplant, peas, carrots, onion and other seasonal products that are mixed, spiced with herbs and pepper, then baked in a clay pot.

Кавърма *(Kavâr'ma)* – chopped pork or lamb stewed with an abundance of onion, mushrooms, tomatoes, etc, and baked in a clay pot.

Кюфте *(Kyuf'te)* – minced pork and veal mixed with finely chopped onion and parsley, shaped as a ball and grilled.

Кебапче *(Ke'bapche)* – rissoles prepared and cooked as the *Kyufte.*

Мусака *(Musa'ka)* – minced pork or veal, diced potatoes, finely chopped onion and parsley, pepper and salt, covered with a mixture of eggs and yogurt, then baked in the oven.

Дроб сарма *(Drop sar'ma)* – finely chopped and boiled lamb's liver mixed with rice and onion, covered with a mixture of eggs and yogurt, and baked in the oven.

DESSERTS

Баклава *(Bakla'va)* – flaky pastry, walnuts, butter and cinnamon, baked in the oven and soaked in sugar syrup.

Menu Highlights

- **Халва** *(Hal'va)* – made of melted butter, sugar, sesame flour, cinnamon, crushed nuts and water.
- **Крем карамел** *(Krem kara'mel)* – eggs, milk and browned sugar, baked in the oven.
- **Кисело мляко с горски плодове** *('Kiselo 'mlyako s 'gorski plodo've)* – sweetened yogurt served with an assortment of forest fruits.

Food

Bread	*Hlyap*	Хляб
rye	*'râzhen*	ръжен
wholemeal	*pâlno'zârnest*	пълнозърнест

Soups	*'Supi*	Супи
bean soup	*bop chor'ba*	боб чорба
chicken soup	*'pileshka 'supa*	пилешка супа
fish soup	*'ribena chor'ba*	рибена чорба
tripe soup	*shkem'be chor'ba*	шкембе чорба
vegetable soup	*zelen'chukova 'supa*	зеленчукова супа

Vegetables	*Zelen'chutsi*	Зеленчуци
beet	*tsvek'lo*	цвекло
Brussels sprouts	*'bryukselskc 'zele*	брюкселско зеле

cabbage	*'zele*	зеле
carrot	*'morkof*	морков
celery	*'tselina*	целина
cucumber	*'krastavitsa*	краставица
eggplant	*patla'dzhan*	патладжан
French beans	*ze'len fa'sul*	зелен фасул
garlic	*'chesân*	чесън
haricot beans	*byal bop*	бял боб
leek	*pras*	праз
lettuce	*ma'rulya*	маруля
mushrooms	*'gâbi*	гъби
olives	*mas'lini*	маслини
onion	*luk*	лук
peas	*grah*	грах
pepper	*'chushka*	чушка
potato	*kar'tof*	картоф
radish	*'repichka*	репичка
spinach	*spa'nak*	спанак
tomato	*do'mat*	домат
zucchini	*'tikvichki*	тиквички

FRUITS	*PLODO'VE*	ПЛОДОВЕ
almonds	*ba'demi*	бадеми
apple	*'yabâlka*	ябълка
apricot	*kay'sia*	кайсия
banana	*ba'nan*	банан
blackberry	*kâ'pina*	къпина
blueberry	*boro'vinka*	боровинка

FOOD

cherry	*che'resha*	череша
fig	*smo'kinya*	смокиня
grapefruit	*'greypfrut*	грейпфрут
grapes	*'grozde*	грозде
hazelnuts	*'leshnitsi*	лешници
lemon	*li'mon*	лимон
melon	*'pâpesh*	пъпеш
orange	*porto'kal*	портокал
peach	*'praskova*	праскова
peanuts	*fâs'tâtsi*	фъстъци
pear	*'krusha*	круша
pineapple	*ana'nas*	ананас
plum	*'sliva*	слива
quince	*'dyulya*	дюля
raisins	*sta'fidi*	стафиди
raspberry	*ma'lina*	малина
sour cherry	*'vishna*	вишна
strawberry	*'yagoda*	ягода
tangerine	*manda'rina*	мандарина
walnuts	*'orehi*	орехи
watermelon	*'dinya*	диня

Pulses — *'Bobovi ras'tenia* — Бобови растения

French beans	*ze'len fa'sul*	зелен фасул
haricot beans	*bop*	боб
lentils	*'leshta*	леща
peas	*grah*	грах

CHEESES AND DESSERTS	*SIRE'NA I DE'SERTI*	СИРЕНА И ДЕСЕРТИ
cake	*'torta/keks*	торта/кекс
cheese	*'sirene*	сирене
cream	*krem*	крем
curds	*iz'vara*	извара
honey	*met*	мед
ice-cream	*slado'let*	сладолед
pancake stuffed with cheese	*pala'chinka sâs 'sirene*	палачинка със сирене
pancake with a chocolate filling	*pala'chinka s shoko'lat*	палачинка с шоколад
pancake stuffed with honey and walnuts	*pala'chinka s met i 'orehi*	палачинка с мед и орехи
sweet	*bon'bon*	бонбон
yellow cheese	*kashka'val*	кашкавал

SEAFOOD	*'MORSKI 'DAROVE*	МОРСКИ ДАРОВЕ
crab	*rak*	рак
herring	*'heringa*	херинга
lobster	*o'mar*	омар
mackerel	*skum'ria*	скумрия
octopus	*okto'pot*	октопод
salmon	*'syomga*	сьомга
shark	*a'kula*	акула
shrimp	*ska'rida*	скарида
trout	*pâs'târva*	пъстърва
fried	*'pârzhena*	пържена
grilled	*na 'skara*	на скара

tuna	*'riba ton*	риба тон
turbot	*kal'kan*	калкан

Meat and Game | *Me'so i 'divech* | Месо и дивеч

beef	*go'vezhdo*	говеждо
brains	*'mozâk*	мозък
chicken	*'pileshko*	пилешко
chicken liver	*'pileshki drop*	пилешки дроб
deer	*e'len*	елен
duck	*'patitsa*	патица
fillet	*fi'le*	филе
hare	*div 'zaek*	див заек
hen	*ko'koshka*	кокошка
lamb	*'agneshko*	агнешко
leg of pork	*'svinski but*	свински бут
loin	*'ribitsa, ka're*	рибица, каре
meatballs	*kyuf'teta*	кюфтета
mince	*kay'ma*	кайма
partridge	*'yarebitsa*	яребица
pork	*'svinsko*	свинско
pork liver	*'svinski drop*	свински дроб
pork chop	*'svinska pâr'zhola*	свинска пържола
roedeer	*sâr'na*	сърна
schnitzel	*'shnitsel*	шницел
tongue	*e'zik*	език
turkey	*'puyka*	пуйка
veal	*'teleshko*	телешко

DRINKS

НАПИТКИ

WATER	***VO'DA***	**ВОДА**
mineral	*mine'ralna*	минерална
sparkling	*ga'zirana*	газирана
tap	*chesh'myana*	чешмяна

COFFEE	***KA'FE***	**КАФЕ**
decaffeinated	*bes kofe'in*	без кофеин
espresso	*es'preso*	еспресо
instant	*'neska'fe*	нескафе
long	*'dâlgo*	дълго
short	*'kâso*	късо
with cream	*sâs sme'tana*	със сметана
with milk	*s 'mlyako*	с мляко
with sugar	*sâs 'zahar*	със захар
without sugar	*bez 'zahar*	без захар

TEA	***CHAY***	**ЧАЙ**
with honey	*s met*	с мед
with lemon	*s li'mon*	с лимон
with milk	*s 'mlyako*	с мляко

Other Non-alcoholic Beverages	*'Drugi bezalko'holni*	Други безалкохолни
buttermilk	*ay'ryan*	айрян
cappuccino	*kapu'chino*	капучино
fresh juice	*fresh*	фреш
hot chocolate	*go'resht shoko'lat*	горещ шоколад
juice	*sok*	сок
milk	*'mlyako*	мляко
millet-ale	*bo'za*	боза

Beer	*'Bira*	Бира
ale/dark	*'tâmna*	тъмна
draught	*na'livna*	наливна
lager	*'svetla*	светла

Wine	*'Vino*	Вино
white	*'byalo*	бяло
red	*cher'veno*	червено
dry	*'suho*	сухо
semi-dry	*po'lu'suho*	полусухо
rose	*ro'ze*	розе
chilled	*ohla'deno*	охладено
champagne/ sparkling wine	*sham'pansko*	шампанско

Spirits	*Alko'holni na'pitki*	Алкохолни напитки
anisette	*mas'tika*	мастика
brandy	*ko'nyak*	коняк
gin	*dzhin*	джин
rum	*rom*	ром
tequila	*te'kila*	текила
vodka	*'votka*	водка
whisky	*u'iski*	уиски

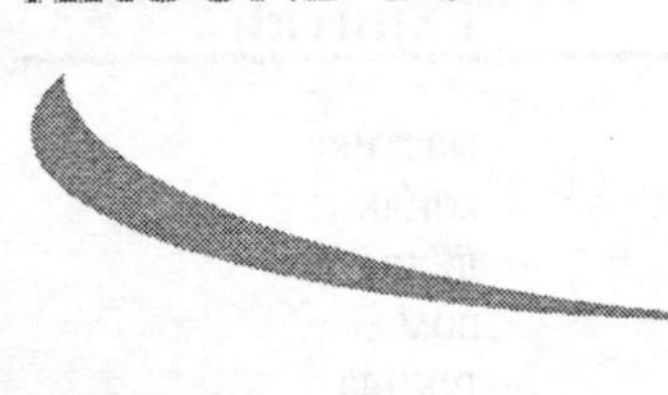

AROUND TOWN

В ГРАДА

DIRECTIONS — PO'SOKI — ПОСОКИ

Directions	Po'soki	Посоки
Turn at the traffic lights/ the corner.	*'Sviyte na sveto'fara/ 'âgâla.*	Свийте на светофара/ ъгъла.
straight ahead	*fse nap'ravo*	все направо
to the left	*na'lyavo*	наляво
to the right	*na'dyasno*	надясно
behind	*zat*	зад
east	*'istok*	изток
far	*da'lech*	далеч
in front of	*pret*	пред
near	*'blizo*	близо
next to	*do*	до
north	*'sever*	север
opposite	*sre'shtu*	срещу
south	*yuk*	юг
west	*'zapat*	запад

SIGNS — 'ZNATSI — ЗНАЦИ

Signs	'Znatsi	Знаци
Closed	*Zat'voreno*	Затворено
Entrance	*Fhot*	Вход

Exit	*'Is-hot*	Изход
Information	*Infor'matsia*	Информация
No vacancies	*'Nyama svo'bodni mes'ta*	Няма свободни места
Open	*Ot'voreno*	Отворено
Police station	*Poli'tseysko uprav'lenie*	Полицейско управление
Prohibited	*Zabra'neno*	Забранено
St/Blvd/Sq	*'Ulitsa/Bule'vart/ Plo'shtat*	Ул./Бул./ Пл.
Toilets	*Toa'letni*	Тоалетни
Men	*Mâ'zhe*	Мъже
Women	*Zhe'ni*	Жени

EMERGENCIES — *'SPESHNI 'SLUCHAI* — СПЕШНИ СЛУЧАИ

Help!	*'Pomosht!*	Помощ!
Fire! Call the fire brigade!	*Po'zhar! Po'vikayte po'zharnata!*	Пожар! Повикайте пожарната!
Call a doctor!	*Po'vikayte 'doktor!*	Повикайте доктор!
Call an ambulance!	*Po'vikayte li'neyka!*	Повикайте линейка!
Call the police!	*Po'vikayte po'litsiata!*	Повикайте полицията!
Go away!	*'Mahay se!*	Махай се!
I'm lost!	*Za'gubih se!*	Загубих се!

Shopping	*Paza'ruvane*	Пазаруване
Where can I buy...?	*Otkâ'de 'moga da 'kupya...?*	Откъде мога да купя...?
Is there nearby a/an...?	*'Ima li nab'lizo...?*	Има ли наблизо...?
antique shop	*antik'varen maga'zin*	антикварен магазин
baby store	*'bebeshki maga'zin*	бебешки магазин
bookstore	*kni'zharnitsa*	книжарница
clothing store	*maga'zin za oblek'lo*	магазин за облекло
department store	*univer'salen maga'zin*	универсален магазин
florist's	*tsve'tarski maga'zin*	цветарски магазин
jeweller's	*zla'tarsko ateli'e*	златарско ателие
market	*pa'zar*	пазар
music store	*muzi'kalen maga'zin*	музикален магазин
newsstand/kiosk	*'butka za 'vesnitsi*	будка за вестници
perfumery and cosmetics shop	*parfyu'meria i koz'metika*	парфюмерия и козметика
pharmacy	*ap'teka*	аптека
photographic shop	*foto'grafsko ateli'e*	фотографско ателие
shoe store	*maga'zin za o'bufki*	магазин за обувки
I'm just looking.	*'Samo 'gledam.*	Само гледам.
How much is this?	*'Kolko 'struva to'va?*	Колко струва това?
How much is it in dollars/euros/pounds?	*'Kolko 'struva to'va v 'dolari/'evro/bri'tanski 'liri?*	Колко струва това в долари/евро/британски лири?

Around Town

It's very expensive.	*'Mnogo e 'skâpo.*	Много е скъпо.
Have you got anything cheaper?	*'Imate li 'neshto 'po-'eftino?*	Имате ли нещо по-евтино?
Write the price down, please.	*Napi'shete mi tse'nata, 'molya.*	Напишете ми цената, моля.

SOUVENIRS	*SUVE'NIRI*	СУВЕНИРИ
I'd like to buy a souvenir.	*'Iskam da 'kupya suve'nir.*	Искам да купя сувенир.
I'm looking for something typical of this region/ Bulgaria.	*'Târsya (da 'kupya) 'neshto ti'pichno za 'tozi kray/ za Bâl'garia.*	Търся (да купя) нещо типично за този край/ за България.
How much?	*'Kolko 'struva?*	Колко струва?

HANDICRAFT	*ZANA'YATI*	ЗАНАЯТИ
bowl	*'kupa*	купа
crystal	*kris'tal*	кристал
embroidery	*bro'deria*	бродерия
glass	*stâk'lo*	стъкло
lace	*dan'tela*	дантела
porcelain	*portse'lan*	порцелан
pottery	*ke'ramika*	керамика
vase	*'vaza*	ваза
wallet	*portmo'ne*	портмоне

CLOTHING | *OBLEK'LO* | ОБЛЕКЛО

I'm looking for...	*'Târsya...*	Търся...
I wear size...	*'Nosya raz'mer...*	Нося размер...
Can I have a look at this?	*'Mozhe li da 'vidya to'va?*	Може ли да видя това?
Can I try this on?	*'Mozhe li da go 'probvam?*	Може ли да го пробвам?
Where's the changing room?	*Kâ'de e 'probnata?*	Къде е пробната?
Do you have this in a larger/smaller size?	*'Imate li 'po-go'lyam/ 'po-'malâk raz'mer?*	Имате ли по-голям/ по-малък размер?
Do you have this in another colour?	*'Imate li to'va v druk tsvyat?*	Имате ли това в друг цвят?
I'll take it.	*Shte go 'vzema.*	Ще го взема.
coat	*pal'to*	палто
dress	*'roklya*	рокля
jacket	*'yake*	яке
jacket (of suit)	*sa'ko*	сако
jeans	*'dzhinsi/'dânki*	джинси/дънки
shirt	*'riza*	риза
skirt	*po'la*	пола
socks	*'kâsi cho'rapi*	къси чорапи
stockings	*'damski cho'rapi*	дамски чорапи
suit	*kos'tyum*	костюм

swimsuit	*'banski (kos'tyum)*	бански (костюм)
tie	*vrato'vrâska*	вратовръзка
tracksuit	*'antsuk*	анцуг
trousers/pants	*panta'lon*	панталон
T-shirt	*'teniska*	тениска
underwear	*be'lyo*	бельо

Sizes	*Raz'meri*	Размери
big	*go'lyam*	голям
small	*'malâk*	малък
narrow	*'tesen*	тесен
wide	*shi'rok*	широк
short	*kâs*	къс
long	*'dâlâk*	дълъг
a little...	*'malko...*	малко...
rather...	*preka'leno...*	прекалено...

Fabrics	*Ma'terii*	Материи
cotton	*pa'muk*	памук
lace	*dan'tela*	дантела
leather	*'kozha*	кожа
artificial	*is'kustvena*	изкуствена
genuine	*es'testvena*	естествена
nylon	*nay'lon*	найлон
silk	*kop'rina*	коприна
suede	*ve'lur*	велур
velvet	*kadi'fe*	кадифе
wool	*'vâlna*	вълна

Colours	*Tsveto've*	Цветове
beige	*'bezhof*	бежов
black	*'cheren*	черен
blue	*sin*	син
brown	*ka'fyaf*	кафяв
dark	*'tâmen*	тъмен
gray	*sif*	сив
green	*ze'len*	зелен
light	*'svetâl*	светъл
orange	*o'ranzhef*	оранжев
pink	*'rozof*	розов
purple	*vio'letof*	виолетов
red	*cher'ven*	червен
white	*byal*	бял
yellow	*zhâlt*	жълт

Shoes	*O'bufki*	Обувки
I wear size...	*'Nosya 'nomer...*	Нося номер...
Can I try on the shoes in the window?	*'Mozhe li da 'probvam o'bufkite ot vit'rinata?*	Може ли да пробвам обувките от витрината?
I'm looking for...	*'Târsya...*	Търся...
formal shoes.	*ofitsi'alni o'bufki.*	официални обувки.
high-heeled shoes.	*o'bufki s vi'sok tok.*	обувки с висок ток.
low-heeled shoes.	*o'bufki s 'nisâk tok.*	обувки с нисък ток.
sports shoes.	*'sportni o'bufki.*	спортни обувки.
summer shoes.	*'letni o'bufki.*	летни обувки.

winter shoes.	*'zimni o'bufki.*	зимни обувки.
boots.	*bo'tushi.*	ботуши.
flip-flops.	*'dzhapanki.*	джапанки.
sandals.	*san'dali.*	сандали.
shoelaces.	*'vrâski za o'bufki.*	връзки за обувки.
shoe polish.	*bo'ya za o'bufki.*	боя за обувки.
slippers.	*pan'tofi.*	пантофи.
Do you have these in a larger/smaller size?	*'Imate li 'po-go'lyam/ 'po-'malâk raz'mer?*	Имате ли по-голям/ по-малък размер?
These are...	*'Tezi sa mi...*	Тези са ми...
a little narrow.	*'malko 'tesni.*	малко тесни.
a little wide.	*'malko shi'roki.*	малко широки.
a little big.	*'malko go'lemi.*	малко големи.
a little small.	*'malki.*	малки.

Photography | *Foto'grafia* | Фотография

I'd like this film processed.	*'Iskam da proya'vite 'tozi film.*	Искам да проявите този филм.
When will it be ready?	*Ko'ga shte 'bâde go'tof?*	Кога ще бъде готов?
I want a roll of 24-/ 36-exposure colour film.	*'Iskam 'tsveten film s 'dvayset i 'chetiri/ 'triyset i shes 'pozi.*	Искам цветен филм с двадесет и четири/ тридесет и шест пози.
camera	*'fotoapa'rat*	фотоапарат
colour/B&W film	*'tsveten/'cherno-byal film*	цветен/черно-бял филм
copy	*'kopie*	копие

digital camera	*digi'talen 'fotoapa'rat*	дигитален фотоапарат
exposure	*'poza*	поза
flash bulb	*svet'kavitsa*	светкавица
negative	*nega'tif*	негатив
picture	*'snimka*	снимка
processing	*pro'mivane*	промиване
size	*raz'mer*	размер

JEWELLERY	*BIZHU'TERIA*	БИЖУТЕРИЯ
bracelet	*'grivna*	гривна
cuff-links	*râka'veli*	ръкавели
earrings	*obe'tsi*	обеци
gold	*'zlato*	злато
necklace	*koli'e*	колие
pearl	*'perla*	перла
precious stone	*skâpo'tsenen 'kamâk*	скъпоценен камък
ring	*'prâsten*	пръстен
silver	*sreb'ro*	сребро

TOILETRIES	*TOA'LETNI PRINAD'LEZHNOSTI*	ТОАЛЕТНИ ПРИНАДЛЕЖНОСТИ
aftershave	*'aftârsheyf*	афтършейв
bath sponge	*'gâba za 'banya*	гъба за баня
body lotion	*losi'on za 'tyalo*	лосион за тяло
comb	*'greben*	гребен
eau de cologne	*odeko'lon*	одеколон
face cream	*krem za li'tse*	крем за лице

hairbrush	*'chetka za ko'sa*	четка за коса
hair-conditioner	*bal'sam za ko'sa*	балсам за коса
hand cream	*krem za râ'tse*	крем за ръце
nail polish remover	*lakochis'titel*	лакочистител
razor	*samobrâs'nachka*	самобръсначка
razor-blade	*'noshche za 'brâsnene*	ножче за бръснене
sanitary napkins	*'damski prev'râski*	дамски превръзки
shampoo	*shampo'an*	шампоан
shaving-brush	*'chetka za 'brâsnene*	четка за бръснене
shaving-foam	*'pyana za 'brâsnene*	пяна за бръснене
shower-gel	*dush-gel*	душ-гел
soap	*sa'pun*	сапун
sunblock milk	*'plazhno 'mlyako*	плажно мляко
tampons	*tam'poni*	тампони
toilet paper	*toa'letna har'tia*	тоалетна хартия
toothbrush	*'chetka za 'zâbi*	четка за зъби
toothpaste	*'pasta za 'zâbi*	паста за зъби

Baby's Needs — *Za 'bebeto* — За бебето

baby food	*hra'na za 'bebeta*	храна за бебета
baby powder	*'bebeshka 'pudra*	бебешка пудра
baby shampoo	*'bebeshki shampo'an*	бебешки шампоан
baby soap	*'bebeshki sa'pun*	бебешки сапун
baby's pot	*'bebeshko gâr'ne*	бебешко гърне
bib	*'ligavniche*	лигавниче
disposable nappies	*'pampersi*	памперси
feeding-bottle	*shi'she za 'mlyako*	шише за мляко
pacifier	*bibe'ron*	биберон

PUBLICATIONS	*PE'CHATNI IZ'DANIA*	ПЕЧАТНИ ИЗДАНИЯ
Do you sell English newspapers/ magazines?	*Pro'davate li an'gliyski 'vesnitsi/ spi'sania?*	Продавате ли английски вестници/ списания?
Do you have an English-Bulgarian dictionary?	*'Imate li an'gliysko-'bâlgarski 'rechnik?*	Имате ли английско-български речник?
Do you have a road map of Bulgaria in English?	*'Imate li 'pâtna 'karta na Bâl'garia na an'gliyski?*	Имате ли пътна карта на България на английски?
Do you sell English books?	*Pro'davate li an'gliyski 'knigi?*	Продавате ли английски книги?
book	*'kniga*	книга
crime/detective story	*krimina'le*	криминале
dictionary	*'rechnik*	речник
envelope	*plik za pis'mo*	плик за писмо
love story	*lyu'boven ro'man*	любовен роман
magazine	*spi'sanie*	списание
newspaper	*'vesnik*	вестник
road map	*'pâtna 'karta*	пътна карта
science-fiction	*na'uchna fan'tastika*	научна фантастика
stamp	*'poshtenska 'marka*	пощенска марка
thriller	*'trilâr*	трилър
travel guide	*pâtevo'ditel*	пътеводител

Tobacco Shop	*Maga'zin za tsi'gari*	Магазин за цигари
A packet of cigarettes, please.	*Pa'ket/ku'tia tsi'gari, 'molya.*	Пакет/кутия цигари, моля.
Do you have lights?	*'Imate li 'po-'leki tsi'gari?*	Имате ли по-леки цигари?
cigar	*'pura*	пура
cigarettes	*tsi'gari*	цигари
lighter	*za'palka*	запалка
matches	*kib'rit*	кибрит
pipe	*lu'la*	лула
tobacco	*tyu'tyun*	тютюн

At the Post Office

When using a public telephone, make sure you carry with you either a ***Mobika*** *phonecard (for blue phones), or a* ***Bulfon*** *phonecard (for orange phones). You can buy* ***fonokarta*** *at the post offices, railway stations, bus stops and at every street kiosk.*

There are now two GSM operators in Bulgaria – ***Mtel*** *and* ***Globul****, and coverage, even in remote parts of the country, is becoming fuller.*

I want to send a...	*'Iskam da is'pratya...*	Искам да изпратя...
fax.	*faks.*	факс.
letter.	*pis'mo.*	писмо.
parcel.	*ko'let.*	колет.
postcard.	*'poshtenska 'kartichka.*	пощенска картичка.
telegram.	*tele'grama.*	телеграма.

How much is the postcard?	*'Kolko 'struva 'kartichkata?*	Колко струва картичката?
I'd like to call...	*'Iskam da se o'badya do...*	Искам да се обадя до...
The number is...	*'Nomera e...*	Номерът е...
The number's busy.	*'Nomera 'dava za'eto.*	Номерът дава заето.
The line's cut off.	*'Liniata pre'kâsna.*	Линията прекъсна.

Useful Words and Phrases / *Po'lezni 'dumi i 'izrazi* / Полезни думи и изрази

envelope	*plik za pis'mo*	плик за писмо
airmail	*vâz'dushna 'poshta*	въздушна поща
surface mail	*obikno'vena 'poshta*	обикновена поща
registered mail	*prepo'râchana 'poshta*	препоръчана поща
answering machine	*tele'fonen sekre'tar*	телефонен секретар
long-distance call	*iz'vân'gratski 'razgovor*	извънградски разговор
reverse charge/ collect call	*'razgovor za 'chuzhda 'smetka*	разговор за чужда сметка
mailbox	*'poshtenska ku'tia*	пощенска кутия

ENTERTAINMENT

РАЗВЛЕЧЕНИЯ

SIGHTSEEING	*ZABELE'ZHITELNOSTI*	ЗАБЕЛЕЖИТЕЛНОСТИ
Are there any sights to see around here?	*'Ima li zabele'zhitelnosti na'okolo?*	Има ли забележителности наоколо?
What are the main attractions?	*Ko'i sa 'glavnite zabele'zhitelnosti?*	Кои са главните забележителности?
Where's...?	*Kâ'de se na'mira...?*	Къде се намира...?
Could you show me on the map?	*'Bihte li mi po'kazali na 'kartata?*	Бихте ли ми показали на картата?
Can I get there on foot?	*'Moga li da 'stigna pe'sha?*	Мога ли да стигна пеша?
When is... open?	*Ko'ga ot'varya...?*	Кога отваря...?
How much is the entrance fee for the museum?	*'Kolko 'struva 'fhoda za mu'zeya?*	Колко струва входът за музея?

What's this building?	*Kak'va e 'tazi 'zgrada/ pos'troyka?*	Каква е тази сграда/ постройка?
How old is it?	*Na 'kolko go'dini e?*	На колко години е?
Can I take pictures?	*'Moga li da 'pravya 'snimki?*	Мога ли да правя снимки?
Do you have an English-speaking guide?	*'Ima li ekskurzo'vot na an'gliyski?*	Има ли екскурзовод на английски?

Art | *Is'kustvo* | Изкуство

Art	*Is'kustvo*	Изкуство
altarpiece	*ikono'stas*	иконостас
amphitheatre	*amfite'atâr*	амфитеатър
art gallery	*hu'dozhestvena ga'leria*	художествена галерия
cathedral	*kate'drala*	катедрала
chapel	*pa'raklis*	параклис
church	*'tsârkva*	църква
catholic	*kato'licheska*	католическа
orthodox	*pravo'slavna*	православна
concert-hall	*kon'tsertna 'zala*	концертна зала
exhibition	*iz'lozhba*	изложба
fortress	*'krepost*	крепост
icon	*i'kona*	икона
monastery	*manas'tir*	манастир
monument	*'pametnik*	паметник
mosque	*dzha'mia*	джамия
museum	*mu'zey*	музей
palace	*dvo'rets*	дворец

park	*park*	парк
sculpture	*skulp'tura*	скулптура

Music | *'Muzika* | Музика

Do you like listening to music?	*O'bichash li da 'slushash 'muzika?*	Обичаш ли да слушаш музика?
What kind of music do you prefer?	*Kak'va 'muzika pretpo'chitash?*	Каква музика предпочиташ?
Which is your favourite band?	*Ko'ya e lyu'bimata ti 'grupa?*	Коя е любимата ти група?
I want to buy some authentic Bulgarian folk music.	*'Iskam da 'kupya aften'tichna 'bâlgarska na'rodna 'muzika.*	Искам да купя автентична българска народна музика.
Do you have the latest album of...?	*'Imate li pos'lednia al'bum na...?*	Имате ли последния албум на...?

Useful Words and Phrases | *Po'lezni 'dumi i 'izrazi* | Полезни думи и изрази

band	*'grupa*	група
concert	*kon'tsert*	концерт
concert-hall	*kon'tsertna 'zala*	концертна зала
disco	*'disko*	диско
folk music	*na'rodna 'muzika*	народна музика

jazz	*dzhas*	джаз
opera	*'opera*	опера
orchestra	*or'kestâr*	оркестър
performance	*pretstav'lenie*	представление
rock	*rok*	рок
singer	*pe'vets/pe'vitsa*	певец *(m)*/певица *(f)*
song	*'pesen*	песен

Cinema and Theatre | *'Kino i te'atâr* | Кино и театър

What's on at the cinema this week?	*Kak'vo 'davat na 'kino 'tazi 'sedmitsa?*	Какво дават на кино тази седмица?
What kind of film?	*Ka'kâf e 'filma?*	Какъв е филмът?
When does it start?	*Ko'ga za'pochva?*	Кога започва?
Are there tickets available for the film?	*'Ima li bi'leti za 'filma?*	Има ли билети за филма?
Who's in the leading part?	*Koy ig'rae v 'glavnata 'rolya?*	Кой играе в главната роля?

Useful Words and Phrases | *Po'lezni 'dumi i 'izrazi* | Полезни думи и изрази

action movie	*'ekshân*	екшън

actor	*ak'tyor*	актьор
actress	*ak'trisa*	актриса
box office	*bi'letna 'kasa*	билетна каса
cinema	*'kino*	кино
comedy	*ko'media*	комедия
director	*rezhi'syor*	режисьор
documentary	*dokumen'talen film*	документален филм
drama	*'drama*	драма
film festival	*'filmof festi'val*	филмов фестивал
horror movie	*film na 'uzhasite*	филм на ужасите
interval	*an'trakt*	антракт
play	*pi'esa*	пиеса
sci-fi movie	*na'uchnofantas'tichen film*	научнофантастичен филм
seat	*'myasto*	място
thriller	*'trilâr*	трилър
tragedy	*tra'gedia*	трагедия

Nightlife

Restaurants are open Monday through Sunday. They close about 12 p.m., but fun seekers can always move to a nightbar or a nightclub, which usually stay open till 4 a.m. In the big cities and the resorts, depending on your preferences or particular mood, you can go to a disco or a nightclub, or you can have a few drinks, while listening to a live performance at a jazz club. Many restaurants (especially the ones along the seaside) offer nice folk programmes worth seeing.

I feel like going to... a bar. a club. a disco.	*'Hodi mi se na...* *bar.* *klup.* *disko'teka.*	Ходи ми се на... бар. клуб. дискотека.
Where can I go for some dancing?	*Kâ'de 'moga da potan'tsuvam?*	Къде мога да потанцувам?
It's on me.	*As 'cherpya.*	Аз черпя.
Same again, please.	*'Oshte ed'no, 'molya.*	Още едно, моля.
How much?	*'Kolko 'struva?*	Колко струва?
Can I have one dance with you?	*'Mozhe li e'din tants?*	Може ли един танц?

IN THE COUNTRY

В ПРОВИНЦИЯТА

Bulgaria provides ample opportunities for both relaxed and active holidays. Traditionally, July and August are the months of summer holidays in Bulgaria. Traffic to the coast rises a few times, and so do prices along the seaside.

A great alternative of the seaside holiday is the fast-developing eco-tourism, as well as guided mountaineering and hiking, which can be really rewarding. If you opt for a less traditional holiday, you can visit the famous ***Dyavolskoto Gârlo*** *(Devil's Throat) and the* ***Yagodina Cave*** *in the Rhodope, or the* ***Magura Cave*** *in Stara Planina. Bird-watching at the* ***Lake Srebârna*** *or on the Black Sea Coast can be a real fun. You could even water-raft in the fast waters of the Iskar river. If you are after mountaineering, Rila, Pirin, Rhodope and Stara Planina will enchant you forever. Of course, don't go without your mountain map (you can get one at every bookstore).*

And finally, you can stay at one of the numerous spa centres (e.g. Velingrad, Hisar, Pamporovo) to relax and rejuvenate your mind and body.

IN THE MOUNTAINS	*F PLANI'NATA*	В ПЛАНИНАТА
Is there a chalet near here?	*'Ima li nab'lizo 'hizha?*	Има ли наблизо хижа?
How far is it to the nearest chalet?	*'Kolko da'lech e 'nay-'bliskata 'hizha?*	Колко далеч е най-близката хижа?
How long is the trail?	*'Kolko 'dâlâk e 'prehoda?*	Колко дълъг е преходът?
Where can I hire mountain gear?	*Otkâ'de 'moga da na'ema pla'ninska ekipi'rofka?*	Откъде мога да наема планинска екипировка?
Where does this path go to?	*Nakâ'de 'vodi 'tazi pâ'teka?*	Накъде води тази пътека?
I need to get to...	*Tryabva da 'stigna do...*	Трябва да стигна до...
I'm lost.	*Za'gubih se.*	Загубих се.
When does it get dark?	*Ko'ga se 'stâmva?*	Кога се стъмва?

USEFUL WORDS AND PHRASES	*PO'LEZNI 'DUMI I 'IZRAZI*	ПОЛЕЗНИ ДУМИ И ИЗРАЗИ
anorak	*'anorak*	анорак
backpack	*'ranitsa*	раница
chalet	*'hizha*	хижа
compass	*kom'pas*	компас

first aid kit	*ap'techka*	аптечка
forest	*go'ra*	гора
hiking boots	*turis'ticheski o'bufki*	туристически обувки
hiking trail	*turis'ticheska pâ'teka*	туристическа пътека
itinerary	*marsh'rut*	маршрут
lake	*'ezero*	езеро
map	*'karta*	карта
marking (winter, summer)	*marki'rofka ('zimna, 'lyatna)*	маркировка (зимна, лятна)
mount	*vrâh*	връх
mountaineer	*plani'nar*	планинар
path	*pâ'teka*	пътека
pocket-knife	*'dzhobno 'noshche*	джобно ножче
refuge	*zas'lon*	заслон
rock climbing	*'skalno ka'terene*	скално катерене
rope	*vâ'zhe*	въже
torch	*fe'nerche*	фенерче
trek	*'prehot*	преход

Camping — *Na 'kâmpink* — На къмпинг

Can we camp here?	*'Mozhe li da lage'ruvame tuk?*	Може ли да лагеруваме тук?
Is there a campsite nearby?	*'Ima li 'kâmpink nab'lizo?*	Има ли къмпинг наблизо?
How much is it per person per night/ per week?	*'Kolko e na cho'vek za ed'na nosht/ ed'na 'sedmitsa?*	Колко е на човек за една нощ/ една седмица?
Can I light a fire here?	*'Moga li da za'palya 'ogân tuk?*	Мога ли да запаля огън тук?

Is there any drinking-water?	*'Ima li pi'teyna vo'da?*	Има ли питейна вода?
Where are the showers/toilets?	*Kâ'de sa 'dushovete/ toa'letnite?*	Къде са душовете/ тоалетните?
Where can I pitch the tent?	*Kâ'de da o'pâna pa'latkata?*	Къде да опъна палатката?

USEFUL WORDS AND PHRASES | *PO'LEZNI 'DUMI I 'IZRAZI* | ПОЛЕЗНИ ДУМИ И ИЗРАЗИ

caravan	*kara'vana*	каравана
cooking utensils	*'pribori i 'sâdove za 'gotvene*	прибори и съдове за готвене
drinking-water	*pi'teyna vo'da*	питейна вода
gas bottle	*'gazova bu'tilka*	газова бутилка
kitchen	*'kuhnya*	кухня
No bonfire!	*'Paleneto na 'ogân zabra'neno!*	Паленето на огън забранено!
No parking!	*Par'kiraneto zabra'neno!*	Паркирането забранено!
per person	*na cho'vek*	на човек
per vehicle	*na ko'la/ pre'vozno 'sretstvo*	на кола/ превозно средство
showers	*'dushove*	душове
sleeping-bag	*'spalen chu'val*	спален чувал
tent	*pa'latka*	палатка
toilets	*toa'letni*	тоалетни
trailer	*remar'ke*	ремарке

At the Seaside	*Na 'morskia bryak*	На морския бряг
Where can I rent an umbrella and a deck-chair?	*Otkâ'de 'moga da na'ema 'plazhen cha'dâr i shez'lonk?*	Откъде мога да наема плажен чадър и шезлонг?
Can I swim here?	*'Mozhe li da se 'pluva tuk?*	Може ли да се плува тук?
Is it safe to swim here?	*Bezo'pasno li e 'pluvaneto tuk?*	Безопасно ли е плуването тук?
How much per hour?	*'Kolko 'struva na chas?*	Колко струва на час?

Useful Words and Phrases	*Po'lezni 'dumi i 'izrazi*	Полезни думи и изрази
boat	*'lotka*	лодка
changing cubicle	*sâble'kalnya*	съблекалня
flip-flops	*'dzhapanki*	джапанки
life jacket	*spa'sitelna zhi'letka*	спасителна жилетка
lifeguard	*spa'sitel*	спасител
paddle boat	*'vodno kole'lo*	водно колело
sunblock	*slântseza'shtiten krem*	слънцезащитен крем
sunglasses	*'slânchevi ochi'la*	слънчеви очила
towel	*hav'lia*	хавлия
water-skiing	*'vodni ski*	водни ски
waves	*vâl'ni*	вълни

SPORTS

Summer sports in Bulgaria include fishing, swimming, scuba-diving and tennis, among others. There's an abundance of fine beaches in Bulgaria, most of which provide everything for the tourist's enjoyment. There are numerous windsurfing schools where you can take lessons, or you could do some kite-surfing or water-skiing.

For winter sports Bulgaria offers some excellently equipped skiing resorts, namely, Pamporovo in the Rhodope Mountains, Borovets in the Rila Mountain, and Bansko in the Pirin Mountain.

SPORTS	*SPOR'TUVANE*	СПОРТУВАНЕ
Is there a football match today?	*'Ima li 'futbolen mach dnes?*	Има ли футболен мач днес?
Who's playing?	*Koy ig'rae?*	Кой играе?
Where's the stadium?	*Kâ'de e stadi'ona?*	Къде е стадионът?

What time does the match start?	*F 'kolko cha'sa za'pochva 'macha?*	В колко часа започва мачът?
How much is the ticket?	*'Kolko 'struva bi'leta?*	Колко струва билетът?
Is there nearby...	*'Ima li nab'lizo...*	Има ли наблизо...
a swimming-pool?	*'pluven ba'seyn?*	плувен басейн?
a tennis-court?	*'teniskort?*	тенискорт?
Where can I hire/ rent...	*Kâ'de 'moga da 'vzema pod 'naem...*	Къде мога да взема под наем...
ski?	*ski?*	ски?
ski boots?	*ski o'bufki?*	ски обувки?
wet suit?	*vodo'lazen kos'tyum?*	водолазен костюм?
I'd like to attend a beginner's/ advanced course in...	*'Iskam da se za'pisha na kurs po... za nachi'naeshti/ nap'rednali.*	Искам да се запиша на курс по... за начинаещи/ напреднали.
Can you play chess/football?	*'Mozhesh li da ig'raesh shah/'futbol?*	Можеш ли да играеш шах/футбол?
Yes, I can/quite well.	*Da, 'moga/'dosta dob're.*	Да, мога/доста добре.
No, not at all.	*Ne, 'nikak.*	Не, никак.
What are the snow conditions like today?	*Kak'vi sa 'snezhnite us'lovia dnes?*	Какви са снежните условия днес?
How much is a daily/ weekly lift pass?	*'Kolko 'struva 'kartata za lift za e'din den/ ed'na 'sedmitsa?*	Колко струва картата за лифт за един ден/ една седмица?

I would like to take skiing lessons.	*'Iskam da 'vzemam u'rotsi po ski.*	Искам да вземам уроци по ски.
When does the lift start?	*Ko'ga 'puskat 'lifta?*	Кога пускат лифта?
Is it very steep?	*'Mnogo li e 'strâmno?*	Много ли е стръмно?

Useful Words and Phrases — *Po'lezni 'dumi i 'izrazi* — Полезни думи и изрази

athletics	*at'letika*	атлетика
ball	*'topka*	топка
basketball	*'basketbol*	баскетбол
bicycle	*kole'lo*	колело
bowling	*'boulink*	боулинг
chair-lift	*se'dalkof lift*	седалков лифт
cycling	*kolo'ezdene*	колоездене
football	*'futbol*	футбол
gymnastics	*gim'nastika*	гимнастика
harpoon	*har'pun*	харпун
horse riding	*ez'da*	езда
player	*ig'rach*	играч
rowing	*'grebane*	гребане
sailing	*vetro'hotstvo*	ветроходство
scuba-diving	*pod'vodno 'gmurkane*	подводно гмуркане
ski-tow	*'ski vlek*	ски влек
snorkel	*'shnorhel*	шнорхел
surfing	*'sârfink*	сърфинг
tennis-racket	*'tenis ra'keta*	тенис ракета
weightlifting	*'vdigane na 'tezhesti*	вдигане на тежести

HOLIDAYS

ПРАЗНИЦИ

National Holidays

1 January – New Year's Day
3 March – Liberation Day
April – Easter
1 May – Labour Day
6 May – Day of Bulgarian Army
24 May – Day of the Slavonic Script and of Bulgarian Education and Culture
6 September – The Unification of Bulgaria
22 September – Independence Day
1 November – Day of the Spiritual Leaders of Bulgaria
24 December – Christmas Eve
25 December – Christmas Day

Orthodox Saints' Days

1 January – Vasilyovden (St. Basil's Day)
6 January – Yordanovden (Epiphany)
7 January – Ivanovden (St. John's Day)
Palm Sunday
Easter
6 May – Gergyovden (St. George's Day)
11 May – St.Cyril and St. Methodius Day
15 August – Golyama Bogoroditsa (The Assumption)
26 October – Dimitrovden (St. Demetrius' Day)
6 December – Nikulden (St. Nicholas' Day)
24 December – Christmas Eve
25 December – Christmas Day

Rough Guide through Bulgarian Folk Customs and Traditions

KUKEROV DEN – This old pagan ritual is performed in early spring (although the date varies from one place to another) to chase away the evil spirits of winter and ensure good harvest. The ritual includes kukerski igri (kukeri games) and processions through the village. It's worth seeing the noisy and merry parade of men dressed up in animal costumes with goat or sheep bells, and wearing wooden masks adorned with multicoloured threads, sequins and small mirrors.

BABA MARTA – Following this Old pagan ritual, on the 1st of March both young and old in Bulgaria put on a martenitsa (made of white and red threads) on their jackets or wrists to bring them health and to keep them from evil spirits. As tradition goes, you are to take the martenitsa off only after seeing a stork. Then you have to put it under a stone or hang it on a tree branch. The person who gave name to this day is Baba Marta (Grandma March). People believe her to be an old grumpy woman, who comes every March to expel Winter. Her unpredictable swings of mood account for the frequent weather changes during this certain month, which may be the reason why men call it the women's month.

Easter *– The traditional greeting on this day (no matter if you are religious or not) is* ***Hristos voskrese!*** *("Christ has risen!"), and the answer's* ***Voistina voskrese!*** *("Indeed has He risen!"). On this day children (and not only) make a contest with eggs. The egg whose shell doesn't crack till the end of the contest wins the name* ***borak*** *(fighter). The traditional meal includes brightly coloured boiled eggs, kozunak and roasted lamb.*

Nikulden (St. Nicholas' Day) *– St. Nicholas is regarded the patron saint of fishermen, sailors and, more recently, bankers. His saint day, Nikulden, is one of the most loved and celebrated Orthodox Church Festivals in Bulgaria. The usual meal on this day is a baked carp stuffed with chopped onion and walnuts.*

Christmas Eve *– On Christmas Eve all members of the family gather round the table for a simple old ritual, which combines both pagan and religious/orthodox elements. The house fills with the heady aroma of incense which is to expel the evil spirits. The meals served on the table have to be simple and vegetarian (Christmas Day marks the end of the pre-Christmas Lent) in respect to God's mother. Equally important is their number, which may be 7, 9 or 11, but odd by all means. The loaf with* ***kasmeti*** *(fortune notes) is most eagerly awaited (especially by children), and the one who gets the piece with the silver coin shall enjoy health and luck during the coming year. A part of the ritual (still practiced in small towns and villages) is burning a* ***badnik*** *(yule-log) in the fireplace. Its burning throughout the night is a promise for health and affluence during the new year.*

*The usual greeting on Christmas Day is **Chestito Rozhdestvo Hristovo!** or **Chestita Koleda!** ("Merry Christmas!"), and **Za mnogo godini!** ("Many happy returns!") at the beginning of the New Year. On January 1st, children go from house to house with **survachka** (cornel tree twigs adorned with popcorn, dried fruit, red woollen threads and cotton) in hand and slap householders on the back, wishing them a healthy and prosperous New Year. In return, the children (called **survakari**) receive fruits, walnuts, sweets and a few coins.*

USEFUL WORDS AND PHRASES	*PO'LEZNI 'DUMI I 'IZRAZI*	ПОЛЕЗНИ ДУМИ И ИЗРАЗИ
Santa Claus	*'Dyado 'Koleda*	Дядо Коледа
Merry Christmas!	*'Vesela 'Koleda!*	Весела Коледа!
Happy New Year!	*Za 'mnogo go'dini!*	За много години!
May you have health and a long life!	*Da si zhif i zdraf!*	Да си жив и здрав!

Birthdays and Name-days

Bulgarians are friendly and hospitable people who know how to enjoy themselves. They use birthdays and name-days as a wonderful opportunity to throw a big and often noisy party. If invited, it's always safe to bring flowers. Just make sure their number is odd.

Birthdays and Name-days	*Rozh'deni i 'imeni dni*	Рождени и именни дни
When's your birthday?	*Ko'ga e rozh'denia ti den?*	Кога е рожденият ти ден?
My birthday is on...	*'Moya rozh'den den e na...*	Моят рожден ден е на...
Happy Birthday!	*Ches'tit rozh'den den!*	Честит рожден ден!
Congratulations!	*Pozdrav'lenia!*	Поздравления!
When's your saint's day?	*Ko'ga e 'imenia ti den?*	Кога е именният ти ден?
Happy Name-day!	*Ches'tit 'imen den!*	Честит имен ден!
Many happy returns!	*Da si zhif/'zhiva i zdraf/'zdrava!*	Да си жив *(m)*/жива *(f)* и здрав *(m)*/здрава *(f)*!

Useful Words and Phrases	*Po'lezni 'dumi i 'izrazi*	Полезни думи и изрази
birthday cake	*'torta*	торта
blow out the candles	*'duham 'sveshtite*	духам свещите
candles	*'sveshti*	свещи
christening	*krâshte'ne*	кръщене
gift	*po'darâk*	подарък
jubilee	*yubi'ley*	юбилей
namesake	*a'dash*	адаш

Weddings	'Svadbi	Сватби
champagne	*sham'pansko*	шампанско
engagement	*go'desh*	годеж
honeymoon	*'meden 'mesets*	меден месец
wedding	*'svadba*	сватба
wedding gift	*'svadben po'darâk*	сватбен подарък
wedding ring	*'brachna hal'ka*	брачна халка
wedding party	*'svadbeno târzhest'vo*	сватбено тържество

Wishes	Pozhe'lania	Пожелания
Good luck!	*Kâs'met!*	Късмет!
Bon voyage!	*Na do'bâr pât!/ Na do'bâr chas!*	На добър път!/ На добър час!
God bless you!	*Naz'drave!*	Наздраве!
Take care!	*Pa'zi se!*	Пази се!

Condolences	Sâbolezno'vania	Съболезнования
My deepest sympathy!	*'Moite 'nay-'iskreni sâbolezno'vania!*	Моите най-искрени съболезнования!

HEALTH

ЗДРАВЕ

Is there a hospital/ dentist near here?	*'Ima li nab'lizo 'bolnitsa/ zâbo'lekarski kabi'net?*	Има ли наблизо болница/ зъболекарски кабинет?
Call an ambulance!	*Po'vikayte li'neyka!*	Повикайте линейка!
It's an emergency!	*'Speshno e!*	Спешно е!
When does the doctor see patients?	*Ko'ga 'lekarya pri'ema patsi'enti?*	Кога лекарят приема пациенти?
Get well soon!	*'Bârzo ozdra'vyavane!*	Бързо оздравяване!

Useful Words and Phrases / *Po'lezni 'dumi i 'izrazi* / Полезни думи и изрази

ambulance	*li'neyka*	линейка
doctor	*'lekar*	лекар
Emergency	*'Bârza 'pomosht*	Бърза помощ
examination	*'preglet*	преглед

health insurance	*'zdravna zastra'hofka*	здравна застраховка
hospital	*'bolnitsa*	болница
nurse	*medi'tsinska ses'tra*	медицинска сестра
polyclinic	*poli'klinika*	поликлиника

AILMENTS	*OP'LAKVANIA*	ОПЛАКВАНИЯ
I feel weak.	*'Chustvam ot'padnalost.*	Чувствам отпадналост.
I feel dizzy.	*'Vie mi se svyat.*	Вие ми се свят.
I feel nauseous.	*Pov'râshta mi se.*	Повръща ми се.
I feel shivery./ I have a fever.	*'Ftrisa me.*	Втриса ме.
I have temperature.	*'Imam tempera'tura.*	Имам температура.
It hurts here.	*Bo'li me tuk.*	Боли ме тук.
I'm allergic to...	*'Imam a'lergia kâm...*	Имам алергия към...
I can't sleep.	*Ne 'moga da spya.*	Не мога да спя.
I'm pregnant.	*'Bremena sâm.*	Бременна съм.

At the Dentist	Pri zâbo'lekarya	При зъболекаря
I have a toothache.	*'Imam zâbo'bol.*	Имам зъбобол.
I've lost a filling.	*'Padna mi 'plomba.*	Падна ми пломба.
My gums hurt/ bleed.	*Bo'lyat me ven'tsite./ Ven'tsite mi kâr'vyat.*	Болят ме венците./ Венците ми кървят.
I need an anaesthetic.	*'Iskam u'poyka.*	Искам упойка.

Useful Words and Phrases	Po'lezni 'dumi i 'izrazi	Полезни думи и изрази
cavity	*'karies*	кариес
dentist	*zâbo'lekar*	зъболекар
filling	*'plomba*	пломба
gums	*ven'tsi*	венци
toothache	*zâbo'bol*	зъбобол
tooth extraction	*'vadene na zâp*	вадене на зъб

At the Pharmacy	F ap'tekata	В аптеката
Is there a 24-hour pharmacy nearby?	*'Ima li nab'lizo deno'noshna ap'teka?*	Има ли наблизо денонощна аптека?
I need something for...	*'Iskam 'neshto za...*	Искам нещо за...

Have you got a prescription?	*'Imate li re'tsepta?*	Имате ли рецепта?
How many times a day?	*'Kolko 'pâti 'dnevno?*	Колко пъти дневно?
Before or after meal?	*Pre'di ili slet 'hranene?*	Преди или след хранене?

antibiotic	*antibio'tik*	антибиотик
chemist	*ap'tekar*	аптекар
condom	*prezerva'tif*	презерватив
contraceptives	*protivoza'chatâchni*	противозачатъчни
homeopathic remedies	*homeopa'tichni le'karstva*	хомеопатични лекарства
pregnancy test	*test za 'bremenost*	тест за бременност
prescription	*re'tsepta*	рецепта
purgative	*purga'tif*	пургатив
remedy for...	*le'karstvo za...*	лекарство за...
sanitary napkins	*'damski prev'râski*	дамски превръзки
sleeping-pills	*prispi'vatelni*	приспивателни
tampons	*'damski tam'poni*	дамски тампони

Parts of the Body	*'Chasti na 'tyaloto*	Части на тялото
ankle	*'glezen*	глезен
appendix	*a'pendiks*	апендикс
arm	*râ'ka*	ръка
back	*grâp*	гръб
bladder	*'pikochen me'hur*	пикочен мехур
blood	*krâf*	кръв

bone	*kost*	кост
breasts	*gâr'di*	гърди
cheek	*'buza*	буза
chest	*'grâden kosh*	гръден кош
chin	*bra'dichka*	брадичка
ear	*u'ho*	ухо
eye	*o'ko*	око
face	*li'tse*	лице
finger	*prâst*	пръст
fingernail	*'nokât*	нокът
foot	*stâ'palo*	стъпало
hair	*ko'sa*	коса
hand	*râ'ka*	ръка
head	*gla'va*	глава
heart	*sâr'tse*	сърце
jaw	*'chelyust*	челюст
kidney	*'bâbrek*	бъбрек
knee	*ko'lyano*	коляно
leg	*krak*	крак
liver	*'cheren drop*	черен дроб
lungs	*'beli 'drobove*	бели дробове
mouth	*us'ta*	уста
muscle	*'muskul*	мускул
neck	*vrat*	врат
nose	*nos*	нос
penis	*'penis*	пенис
rib	*reb'ro*	ребро
shoulder	*'ramo*	рамо
skin	*'kozha*	кожа
spine	*grâb'nachen stâlp*	гръбначен стълб
stomach	*sto'mah*	стомах
thigh	*bed'ro*	бедро

throat	*'gârlo*	гърло
tongue	*e'zik*	език
tonsils	*'slivitsi*	сливици
tooth	*zâp*	зъб
vagina	*'vagina*	вагина
vein	*'vena*	вена

DISEASES | *'BOLESTI* | БОЛЕСТИ

allergy	*a'lergia*	алергия
anaemia	*a'nemia*	анемия
angina tonsillaris	*an'gina*	ангина
appendicitis	*apandi'sit*	апандисит
asthma	*'asma*	астма
bite	*u'hapvane*	ухапване
blood pressure (high, low)	*'krâvno na'lyagane (vi'soko, 'nisko)*	кръвно налягане (високо, ниско)
bronchitis	*bron'hit*	бронхит
burn	*iz'garyane*	изгаряне
cancer	*rak*	рак
cold	*nas'tinka*	настинка
colic	*'koliki*	колики
constipation	*'zapek*	запек
cough	*'kashlitsa*	кашлица
diabetes	*dia'bet*	диабет
diarrhea	*di'aria*	диария
dislocation/sprain	*is'kâlchvane*	изкълчване
ear infection	*o'tit*	отит
fever	*'treska*	треска
fit	*pri'padâk*	припадък
gastritis	*gast'rit*	гастрит

headache	*glavo'bolie*	главоболие
heart attack	*in'farkt*	инфаркт
heartburn	*sto'mashni kiseli'ni*	стомашни киселини
heartstroke	*in'farkt*	инфаркт
heatstroke	*top'linen 'udar*	топлинен удар
hemorrhage	*krâvo'izlif*	кръвоизлив
indigestion	*'losho hrano'smilane*	лошо храносмилане
infection	*in'fektsia*	инфекция
inflammation	*vâspa'lenie*	възпаление
intoxication	*nat'ravyane*	натравяне
peritonitis	*perito'nit*	перитонит
pneumonia	*pnev'monia*	пневмония
poisoning	*ot'ravyane*	отравяне
sneezing	*'kihane*	кихане
sting	*u'zhilvane*	ужилване
sunstroke	*'slânchef 'udar*	слънчев удар
tumour	*'tumor*	тумор
ulcer	*'yazva*	язва
varicose veins	*rasshi'reni 'veni*	разширени вени
vomiting	*pov'râshtane*	повръщане
wound	*'rana*	рана

CONVERSION TABLES

ПРЕВРЪЩАНЕ НА МЕРНИ ЕДИНИЦИ

inches		*mm*	*feet*		*m*
0.039	1	25.4	3.281	1	0.305
0.079	2	50.8	6.562	2	0.610
0.118	3	76.2	9.843	3	0.914
0.157	4	101.6	13.123	4	1.219
0.197	5	127.0	16.404	5	1.524
0.236	6	152.4	19.685	6	1.829
0.276	7	177.8	22.966	7	2.134
0.315	8	203.2	26.247	8	2.435
0.354	9	228.6	29.528	9	2.743

gallons		*litres*	*yards*		*m*
0.220	1	4.544	1.094	1	0.914
0.440	2	9.087	2.187	2	1.829
0.660	3	13.631	3.281	3	2.743
0.880	4	18.174	4.374	4	3.658
1.101	5	22.718	5.468	5	4.572
1.321	6	27.262	6.562	6	5.486
1.541	7	31.805	7.655	7	6.401
1.761	8	36.349	8.749	8	7.315
1.981	9	40.892	9.842	9	8.230

Speed

mph	*20*	*30*	*40*	*50*	*60*	*70*	*80*	*90*	*100*
km/h	*32*	*48*	*64*	*80*	*96*	*112*	*128*	*144*	*160*

Temperature

°F	*32*	*40*	*50*	*60*	*70*	*80*	*90*	*100*	*110*	*120*	*130*	*140*	*150*	*160*	*170*	*180*	*190*	*200*	*212*

°C	*0*	*10*	*20*	*30*	*40*	*50*	*60*	*70*	*80*	*90*	*100*

АДРЕСИ И НОМЕРА

British Embassy in Bulgaria

9 Moskovska Str.
Sofia 1000
Bulgaria
Tel: (+ 359 2) 933-9222
Fax: (+ 359 2) 933-9250
E-mail: britembinf@mail.orbitel.bg
http://www.british-embassy.bg

The US Embassy in Sofia

1 Suborna Str.
Sofia 1000
Bulgaria
Tel: (+ 359 2) 937-5100
General E-mail box: irc@usembassy.bg

Consular Section of the US Embassy

1 Kapitan Andreev Str.
Sofia 1421
Bulgaria
Tel: (+ 359 2) 963-2022

Mini-directory

These are some useful local numbers in Bulgaria. When dialling from outside Bulgaria, you must use your country's international access code and Bulgaria's country code. And be sure to omit the "0" that precedes the city codes.

Bulgaria's country code .... *+ 359*
Fire Emergency *160*
Medical Emergency *150*
Police *166*
Traffic Police *165*
Local Directory Assistance *144*
British Airways .... *(02) 981-70-00*
Lufthansa .... *(02) 980-41-41*
UPS .... *(02) 9-60-96*
DHL .... *(02) 988-23-09*

For more information on Bulgaria you can visit:
www.bulgaria.com
www.travel-bulgaria.com

ENGLISH-BULGARIAN DICTIONARY

A

able	*spo'soben*	способен
about	*za*	за
above	*nat*	над
abroad	*f chuzh'bina*	в чужбина
accelerator	*pe'dal na gas'ta*	педал на газта
accident	*zlopo'luka*	злополука
accommodation	*nasta'nyavane*	настаняване
account	*'smetka*	сметка
ache	*'bolka*	болка
across	*pres*	през
active	*ak'tiven*	активен
actor	*ak'tyor*	актьор
actress	*akt'risa*	актриса
address	*ad'res*	адрес
to admire	*vâs-hi'shtavam se ot*	възхищавам се от
adult	*'vâzrasten*	възрастен
adventure	*priklyu'chenie*	приключение
advertisement	*rek'lama*	реклама
advice	*sâ'vet*	съвет
airplane	*samo'let*	самолет
to afford	*pozvo'lyavam si*	позволявам си
afraid	*is'plashen*	изплашен
to be afraid of	*stra'huvam se ot*	страхувам се от
after	*slet*	след
afternoon	*sle'dobet*	следобед

again	*pak*	пак
against	*sre'shtu*	срещу
age	*'vâzrast*	възраст
ago	*pre'di*	преди
to agree	*sâgla'syavam se*	съгласявам се
agriculture	*zeme'delie*	земеделие
ahead	*nap'ret*	напред
AIDS	*spin*	СПИН
air	*'vâzduh*	въздух
air-conditioner	*klima'tik*	климатик
air-hostess	*styuar'desa*	стюардеса
airport	*le'tishte*	летище
alarm clock	*bu'dilnik*	будилник
album	*al'bum*	албум
alcohol	*alko'hol*	алкохол
all	*'fsichko*	всичко
all right	*dob're*	добре
allergic	*aler'gichen*	алергичен
almost	*poch'ti*	почти
alone	*sam*	сам
alphabet	*'azbuka*	азбука
already	*'veche*	вече
also	*'sâshto*	също
altitude	*nad'morska visochi'na*	надморска височина
always	*'vinagi*	винаги
am: I am	*as sâm*	аз съм
ambassador	*pos'lanik*	посланик
ambulance	*li'neyka*	линейка
ancient	*'dreven*	древен
and	*i*	и
angry	*ya'dosan*	ядосан
animal	*zhi'votno*	животно
ankle	*'glezen*	глезен
anniversary	*go'dishnina*	годишнина
anorak	*'anorak*	анорак
another	*druk*	друг
another drink	*'oshte ed'no piti'e*	още едно питие
answer	*'odgovor*	отговор
to answer	*odgo'varyam*	отговарям
apology	*izvi'nenie*	извинение

appetite	*ape'tit*	апетит
apple	*'yabâlka*	ябълка
apricot	*kay'sia*	кайсия
April	*ap'ril*	април
are:		
you are *sg*	*ti si*	ти си
you are *pl*	*'vie ste*	вие сте
they are	*te sa*	те са
arm	*râ'ka*	ръка
to arrest	*ares'tuvam*	арестувам
arrival	*pris'tigane*	пристигане
art	*is'kustvo*	изкуство
artist	*hu'dozhnik*	художник
ashtray	*pepel'nik*	пепелник
to ask (a question)	*'pitam*	питам
to ask (for something)	*'molya*	моля
aspirin	*aspi'rin*	аспирин
asthma	*'asma*	астма
athletics	*at'letika*	атлетика
atlas	*at'las*	атлас
attention	*vni'manie*	внимание
attract	*priv'licham*	привличам
aubergine	*patla'dzhan*	патладжан
audience	*'publika*	публика
August	*'avgust*	август
aunt	*'lelya*	леля
author	*'aftor*	автор
autumn	*'esen*	есен
awful	*u'zhasen*	ужасен

B

baby	*'bebe*	бебе
back	*grâp*	гръб
backache	*'bolki v gâr'ba*	болки в гърба
backpack	*'ranitsa*	раница
bacon	*be'kon*	бекон

bad	*losh*	лош
bag	*'chanta*	чанта
baggage	*ba'gash*	багаж
bagpipe	*'gayda*	гайда
bait	*strâf*	стръв
to bake	*pe'ka*	пека
balcony	*bal'kon*	балкон
ball	*'topka*	топка
ball-point (pen)	*himi'kalka*	химикалка
banana	*ba'nan*	банан
bandage	*prev'râska*	превръзка
bank	*'banka*	банка
banknote	*bank'nota*	банкнота
bar	*bar*	бар
barber's	*brâs'narnitsa*	бръснарница
bargain	*'zdelka*	сделка
basket	*'koshnitsa*	кошница
bathroom	*'banya*	баня
bathing-suit	*'banski kos'tyum*	бански костюм
battery	*ba'teria*	батерия
beach	*plash*	плаж
beans	*bop*	боб
beard	*bra'da*	брада
beautiful	*kra'sif*	красив
beauty parlour	*kozme'tichen sa'lon*	козметичен салон
because	*za'shtoto*	защото
bed	*leg'lo*	легло
bed linen	*'spalno be'lyo*	спално бельо
bedroom	*'spalnya*	спалня
beef	*go'vezhdo*	говеждо
beer	*'bira*	бира
before	*pre'di*	преди
beginner	*nachi'naesht*	начинаещ
behind	*zat*	зад
begin	*za'pochvam*	започвам
beige	*'bezhof*	бежов
bell (on door)	*zvâ'nets*	звънец
bell (of church)	*kam'bana*	камбана
beside	*do*	до
best man	*kum*	кум
bet	*bas*	бас

between	*mezh'du*	между
bib	*'ligavnik*	лигавник
bicycle	*kole'lo*	колело
big	*go'lyam*	голям
bilingual	*dvue'zichen*	двуезичен
bill	*'smetka*	сметка
bird	*'ptitsa*	птица
birth	*'razhdane*	раждане
birthday	*rozh'den den*	рожден ден
biscuit	*bisk'vita*	бисквита
bitter	*gor'chif*	горчив
black	*'cheren*	черен
blackberry	*kâ'pina*	къпина
blanket	*ode'yalo*	одеяло
to bleed	*kâr'vya*	кървя
blind	*slyap*	сляп
blister	*'prishka*	пришка
blond	*rus*	рус
blood	*krâf*	кръв
blouse	*'bluza*	блуза
blue	*sin*	син
boat	*'lotka*	лодка
body	*'tyalo*	тяло
book	*'kniga*	книга
bookshop	*kni'zharnitsa*	книжарница
boot	*bo'tush*	ботуш
border	*'granitsa*	граница
boring	*'skuchen*	скучен
born	*ro'den*	роден
boss	*shef*	шеф
bottle	*bu'tilka*	бутилка
bottle opener	*otva'rachka*	отварачка
box	*ku'tia*	кутия
boy	*mom'che*	момче
boyfriend	*pri'yatel*	приятел
bra	*suti'en*	сутиен
bracelet	*'grivna*	гривна
brake	*spi'rachka*	спирачка
bread	*hlyap*	хляб
breakfast	*za'kuska*	закуска

DICTIONARY

to breathe	*'disham*	дишам
bridge	*most*	мост
brother	*brat*	брат
brown	*ka'fyaf*	кафяв
building	*'zgrada*	сграда
bulb	*elek'tricheska 'krushka*	електрическа крушка
to burn	*go'rya*	горя
bus	*afto'bus*	автобус
bus stop	*afto'busna 'spirka*	автобусна спирка
business	*'rabota*	работа
busy	*za'et*	зает
but	*no*	но
butter	*mas'lo*	масло
to buy	*ku'puvam*	купувам

C

cabbage	*'zele*	зеле
cable-car lift	*ka'binkof lift*	кабинков лифт
café	*kafe'ne*	кафене
cake	*'torta*	торта
calendar	*kalen'dar*	календар
call (on the telephone)	*o'bazhdane*	обаждане
camera	*'fotoapa'rat*	фотоапарат
campsite	*'kâmpink*	къмпинг
can (be able to)	*'moga*	мога
to cancel	*ot'menyam*	отменям
candle	*svesht*	свещ
capital	*'stolitsa*	столица
car	*ko'la*	кола
car park	*'parkink*	паркинг
card	*'kartichka*	картичка
to play cards	*ig'raya 'karti*	играя карти
carpet	*ki'lim*	килим
carrot	*'morkof*	морков
cash	*pa'ri v broy*	пари в брой
cassette	*ka'seta*	касета

cassette player	*kaseto'fon*	касетофон
castle	*'zamâk*	замък
cat	*'kotka*	котка
cathedral	*kated'rala*	катедрала
catholic (person)	*kato'lik*	католик
cauliflower	*karfi'ol*	карфиол
cave	*peshte'ra*	пещера
celebration	*praznen'stvo*	празненство
centimetre	*santi'metâr*	сантиметър
centre	*'tsentâr*	център
century	*vek*	век
certainly	*raz'bira se*	разбира се
chair	*stol*	стол
change	*pro'myana*	промяна
change (small coins)	*'resto*	ресто
charge	*'taksa*	такса
cheap	*'eftin*	евтин
check	*pro'verka*	проверка
to check in	*regist'riram se*	регистрирам се
cheers!	*naz'drave!*	наздраве!
cheese	*'sirene*	сирене
chef	*'glaven got'vach*	главен готвач
chemist's	*ap'teka*	аптека
cheque	*chek*	чек
cheque-book	*'chekova 'knishka*	чекова книжка
cherry	*che'resha*	череша
chess	*shah*	шах
chest (part of body)	*'grâden kosh*	гръден кош
chest (furniture)	*san'dâk*	сандък
chewing-gum	*'dâfka*	дъвка
chicken	*'pile*	пиле
child	*de'te*	дете
china	*portse'lan*	порцелан
chips	*'pârzheni kar'tofi*	пържени картофи
chocolate	*shoko'lat*	шоколад
choice	*'izbor*	избор
chop	*pâr'zhola*	пържола
Christmas	*'koleda*	Коледа
church	*'tsârkva*	църква
cigar	*'pura*	пура

DICTIONARY

cigarette	*tsi'gara*	цигара
cinema	*'kino*	кино
citizen	*'grazhdanin*	гражданин
city	*grat*	град
clean	*chist*	чист
clerk	*chi'novnik*	чиновник
clever	*'umen*	умен
to climb	*ka'terya se*	катеря се
clock	*cha'sovnik*	часовник
to close	*zat'varyam*	затварям
closed	*zat'voren*	затворен
clothes	*'drehi*	дрехи
cloudy	*'oblachen*	облачен
coast	*bryak*	бряг
coat	*pal'to*	палто
coffee	*ka'fe*	кафе
coin	*mo'neta*	монета
cold	*stu'den*	студен
to have a cold	*nas'tinal sâm*	настинал съм
collection	*ko'lektsia*	колекция
colour	*tsvyat*	цвят
comb	*'greben*	гребен
to come	*'idvam*	идвам
compact disc	*kom'pakt'disk*	компактдиск
compartment (in train)	*ku'pe*	купе
compass	*kom'pas*	компас
competition	*sâste'zanie*	състезание
complaint	*op'lakvane*	оплакване
computer	*kom'pyutâr*	компютър
concert	*kon'tsert*	концерт
conductor (in train)	*kon'duktor*	кондуктор
conductor (of orchestra)	*diri'gent*	диригент
congratulations!	*pozdrav'lenia!*	поздравления!
connection	*'vrâska*	връзка
conversation	*'razgovor*	разговор
cook	*got'vach*	готвач
cooker	*got'varska 'pechka*	готварска печка
copper	*met*	мед
corner	*'âgâl*	ъгъл
corridor	*kori'dor*	коридор

to cost	*'struvam*	струвам
How much does it cost?	*'Kolko 'struva?*	Колко струва?
cotton	*pa'muk*	памук
cough	*'kashlitsa*	кашлица
to count	*bro'ya*	броя
country	*stra'na*	страна
court	*sât*	съд
cousin	*bratof'chet*	братовчед
crab	*rak*	рак
craft	*zana'yat*	занаят
craftsman	*zanayat'chia*	занаятчия
crazy	*lut*	луд
cream (for coffee)	*sme'tana*	сметана
cream (cosmetics)	*krem*	крем
credit card	*'kreditna 'karta*	кредитна карта
crisps	*chips*	чипс
croissant	*kroa'san*	кроасан
cross	*krâst*	кръст
cucumber	*'krastavitsa*	краставица
cup	*'chasha*	чаша
custom	*obi'chay*	обичай
customs	*'mitnitsa*	митница
customs officer	*mitni'char*	митничар
to cut	*'rezha*	режа
cycling	*kolo'ezdene*	колоездене

D

dad	*'tatko*	татко
damage	*shte'ta*	щета
dance	*tants*	танц
danger	*o'pasnost*	опасност
date	*'data*	дата
daughter	*dâshte'rya*	дъщеря
day	*den*	ден
dead	*'mârtâf*	мъртъв
deaf	*gluh*	глух

dear	*skâp*	скъп
December	*de'kemvri*	декември
to declare	*dekla'riram*	декларирам
deep	*dâl'bok*	дълбок
degree	*'gradus*	градус
delay	*zakâs'nenie*	закъснение
dentist	*zâbo'lekar*	зъболекар
departure	*zami'navane*	заминаване
depressed	*u'nil*	унил
description	*opi'sanie*	описание
destination	*naprav'lenie*	направление
diabetic (person)	*diabe'tik*	диабетик
to dial	*na'biram*	набирам
diary	*'dnevnik*	дневник
dice	*'zarove*	зарове
dictionary	*'rechnik*	речник
to die	*u'miram*	умирам
different	*raz'lichen*	различен
difficult	*'truden*	труден
dining-room	*trape'zaria*	трапезария
dinner	*ve'cherya*	вечеря
direction	*po'soka*	посока
directory	*tele'fonen uka'zatel*	телефонен указател
dirty	*'mrâsen*	мръсен
disabled	*inva'lit*	инвалид
disco	*disko'teka*	дискотека
disease	*'bolest*	болест
distance	*rasto'yanie*	разстояние
district	*'oblast*	област
to disturb	*bespoko'ya*	безпокоя
diving	*'gmurkane*	гмуркане
divorced	*raz'veden*	разведен
to do	*'pravya, 'vârsha*	правя, върша
doctor	*'lekar*	лекар
document	*doku'ment*	документ
dog	*'kuche*	куче
doll	*'kukla*	кукла
dome	*ku'be*	кубе
door	*vra'ta*	врата
double	*'dvoen*	двоен

down	*'dolu*	долу
dozen	*du'zina*	дузина
dress	*'roklya*	рокля
to drink	*'pia*	пия
to drive	*sho'firam*	шофирам
driver	*sho'fyor*	шофьор
driving-licence	*sho'fyorska 'knishka*	шофьорска книжка
to drizzle	*râ'mya*	ръмя
dry	*suh*	сух
dustbin	*'kofa za smet*	кофа за смет
duty-free	*bez'miten*	безмитен

E

ear; ears	*u'ho; u'shi*	ухо; уши
earache	*uho'bol*	ухобол
early	*'rano*	рано
earrings	*obe'tsi*	обеци
earthquake	*zemetre'senie*	земетресение
east	*'istok*	изток
easy	*'lesen*	лесен
to eat	*yam*	ям
ecology	*eko'logia*	екология
egg	*yay'tse*	яйце
eight	*'osem*	осем
eighteen	*osem'nayset*	осемнайсет
eighty	*osemde'set*	осемдесет
elbow	*'lakât*	лакът
election	*'izbori*	избори
electrician	*elektroteh'nik*	електротехник
electricity	*tok*	ток
elevator	*asan'syor*	асансьор
eleven	*edi'nayset*	единайсет
embassy	*po'solstvo*	посолство
embroidery	*bro'deria*	бродерия
empty	*'prazen*	празен
end	*kray*	край

engine (of a car)	*dvi'gatel*	двигател
enough	*dos'tatâchno*	достатъчно
entry	*fhot*	вход
envelope	*plik za pis'mo*	плик за писмо
environment	*o'kolna sre'da*	околна среда
equipment	*ekipi'rofka*	екипировка
error	*'greshka*	грешка
evening	*'vecher*	вечер
event	*sâ'bitie*	събитие
every	*'fseki*	всеки
everybody	*'fsichki*	всички
everything	*'fsichko*	всичко
everywhere	*naf'syakâde*	навсякъде
exactly	*'tochno*	точно
excess baggage	*'svrâhba'gash*	свръхбагаж
exchange rate	*ob'menen kurs*	обменен курс
excuse me!	*izvi'nete!*	извинете!
exhibition	*iz'lozhba*	изложба
exit	*'is-hot*	изход
expensive	*skâp*	скъп
eye; eyes	*o'ko; o'chi*	око; очи

F

face	*li'tse*	лице
fact	*fakt*	факт
in fact	*'fsâshnost*	всъщност
fair	*pana'ir*	панаир
family	*se'meystvo*	семейство
famous	*pro'chut*	прочут
fan	*zapa'lyanko*	запалянко
far	*da'lech*	далеч
How far is...?	*'Kolko da'lech e...?*	Колко далеч е...?
farm	*'ferma*	ферма
fashion	*'moda*	мода
fast	*bârs*	бърз

father	*ba'shta*	баща
fear	*strah*	страх
February	*fevru'ari*	февруари
to feel	*'chustvam*	чувствам
fiancé	*gode'nik*	годеник
fiancée	*gode'nitsa*	годеница
field	*po'le*	поле
fifteen	*pet'nayset*	петнайсет
fifty	*pede'set*	петдесет
to fill in	*po'pâlvam*	попълвам
filling (in cake)	*'plânka*	плънка
filling (in tooth)	*'plomba*	пломба
film	*film*	филм
finally	*nak'raya*	накрая
to find	*na'miram*	намирам
finger	*prâst*	пръст
to finish	*'svârshvam*	свършвам
fire	*'ogân*	огън
fire-engine	*po'zharna ko'la*	пожарна кола
fireman	*pozharni'kar*	пожарникар
first	*prâf*	пръв
first aid kit	*ap'techka*	аптечка
fish	*'riba*	риба
five	*pet*	пет
fizzy	*ga'ziran*	газиран
flag	*'zname*	знаме
flash (of camera)	*svet'kavitsa*	светкавица
flat	*aparta'ment*	апартамент
flavour	*fkus*	вкус
flight	*'polet*	полет
flip-flops	*'dzhapanki*	джапанки
floor (in a building)	*e'tash*	етаж
floor (ground)	*pot*	под
flour	*brash'no*	брашно
flower	*'tsvete*	цвете
flu	*grip*	грип
fog	*mâg'la*	мъгла
foggy	*mâg'lif*	мъглив
folk music	*na'rodna 'muzika*	народна музика
food	*hra'na*	храна

foot	*stâ'palo*	стъпало
for	*za*	за
forecast	*prog'noza*	прогноза
foreigner	*chuzhde'nets*	чужденец
forest	*go'ra*	гора
forever	*za'vinagi*	завинаги
to forget	*zab'ravyam*	забравям
fork	*'vilitsa*	вилица
form (document)	*formu'lyar*	формуляр
fortress	*'krepost*	крепост
forty	*che'tiriyset*	четирийсет
four	*'chetiri*	четири
fourteen	*chetiri'nayset*	четиринайсет
free (not busy)	*svo'boden*	свободен
free (no charge)	*bes'platen*	безплатен
to freeze	*zam'râzvam*	замръзвам
Friday	*'petâk*	петък
fridge	*hla'dilnik*	хладилник
friend	*pri'yatel*	приятел
from	*ot*	от
fruit	*plot*	плод
full	*'pâlen*	пълен
furniture	*'mebeli*	мебели

G

game	*ig'ra*	игра
garage	*ga'rash*	гараж
garden	*gra'dina*	градина
garlic	*'chesân*	чесън
gas	*gas*	газ
gate	*'porta*	порта
gear	*'skorosna ku'tia*	скоростна кутия
to get	*polu'chavam*	получавам
to get off (a bus)	*'slizam ot*	слизам от
to get on (a bus)	*'kachvam se na*	качвам се на
to get up (from bed)	*'stavam ot*	ставам от

gift	*po'darâk*	подарък
gypsy	*'tsiganin*	циганин
girl	*mo'miche*	момиче
girlfriend	*pri'yatelka*	приятелка
to give	*'davam*	давам
glad	*'radosten*	радостен
glass (material)	*stâk'lo*	стъкло
glass (for drinking)	*'chasha*	чаша
glasses	*ochi'la*	очила
gloves	*râka'vitsi*	ръкавици
glue	*le'pilo*	лепило
to go	*o'tivam*	отивам
gold	*'zlato*	злато
good	*do'bâr*	добър
goodbye	*do'vizhdane*	довиждане
government	*pra'vitelstvo*	правителство
grandchildren	*'vnutsi*	внуци
grandfather	*'dyado*	дядо
grandmother	*'baba*	баба
grapes	*'grozde*	грозде
grass	*tre'va*	трева
great	*ve'lik*	велик
green	*ze'len*	зелен
grey	*sif*	сив
grill	*'skara*	скара
guard	*oh'rana*	охрана
guest	*gost*	гост
guide	*ekskurzo'vot*	екскурзовод
guidebook	*pâtevo'ditel*	пътеводител
guitar	*ki'tara*	китара

H

hair	*ko'sa*	коса
hairdresser	*fri'zyor*	фризьор
hair-dryer	*sesho'ar*	сешоар
ham	*'shunka*	шунка

hamburger	*'hamburger*	хамбургер
hand	*râ'ka*	ръка
handkerchief	*'nosna 'kârpa*	носна кърпа
handsome	*kra'sif*	красив
hang-gliding	*'deltaplane'rizâm*	делтапланеризъм
hangover	*mahmur'luk*	махмурлук
happy	*shtas'lif*	щастлив
harbour	*pris'tanishte*	пристанище
hard (solid)	*tvârt*	твърд
hard (difficult)	*'truden*	труден
hat	*'shapka*	шапка
to have	*'imam*	имам
to have breakfast	*za'kusvam*	закусвам
to have dinner	*ve'cheryam*	вечерям
to have lunch	*o'byadvam*	обядвам
have to	*'tryabva*	трябва
he	*toy*	той
head	*gla'va*	глава
headache	*glavo'bolie*	главоболие
health	*'zdrave*	здраве
to hear	*'chuvam*	чувам
heart	*sâr'tse*	сърце
heat	*'zhega*	жега
heating	*otop'lenie*	отопление
heavy	*'tezhâk*	тежък
hello	*zdra'vey*	здравей
help	*'pomosht*	помощ
her	*'nein*	неин
herb	*'bilka*	билка
here	*tuk*	тук
hi!	*'zdrasti*	здрасти
high	*vi'sok*	висок
highway	*magist'rala*	магистрала
hill	*hâlm*	хълм
to hire	*na'emam*	наемам
his	*'negof*	негов
hobby	*'hobi*	хоби
holiday	*'praznik*	празник
holidays	*va'kantsia*	ваканция
home	*dom*	дом

honey	*'pchelen met*	пчелен мед
horse	*kon*	кон
hospital	*'bolnitsa*	болница
hostel	*opshte'zhitie*	общежитие
hot	*go'resht*	горещ
hotel	*ho'tel*	хотел
hour	*chas*	час
per hour	*f chas, na chas*	в час, на час
house	*'kâshta*	къща
how	*kak*	как
how (many, much)	*'kolko*	колко
hundred	*sto*	сто
hungry	*'gladen*	гладен
husband	*sâp'ruk*	съпруг
hut	*'hizha; ko'liba*	хижа; колиба

I

I	*as*	аз
ice	*let*	лед
ice-cream	*slado'let*	сладолед
if	*ak'o*	ако
ignition (of engine)	*za'palvane*	запалване
ill	*'bolen*	болен
important	*'vazhen*	важен
impossible	*nevâz'mozhen*	невъзможен
impressive	*vnu'shitelen*	внушителен
improvement	*podob'renie*	подобрение
in	*v(âf)*	в(ъв)
income	*'dohot*	доход
indicator	*bro'yach*	брояч
industry	*pro'mishlenost*	промишленост
information	*infor'matsia*	информация
inside	*'vâtre*	вътре
insurance	*zastra'hofka*	застраховка
to be interested in	*intere'suvam se ot*	интересувам се от
international	*mezhduna'roden*	международен

Internet	*'internet*	Интернет
invitation	*po'kana*	покана
is:	*e*	е
he is	*toy e*	той е
she is	*tya e*	тя е
it is	*to e*	то е
island	*'ostrof*	остров
it	*to*	то
itch	*sâr'besh*	сърбеж
ivory	*'slonova kost*	слонова кост

J

jacket	*'yake*	яке
jail	*zat'vor*	затвор
jam	*konfi'tyur*	конфитюр
January	*yanu'ari*	януари
jeans	*'dzhinsi*	джинси
jellyfish	*me'duza*	медуза
jewellery	*bi'zhuta*	бижута
job	*'rabota*	работа
jogging	*'dzhogink*	джогинг
joke	*she'ga*	шега
journey	*pâte'shestvie*	пътешествие
juice	*sok*	сок
July	*'yuli*	юли
June	*'yuni*	юни

K

to keep	*'pazya*	пазя
kettle	*'chaynik*	чайник
key	*klyuch*	ключ
kidney	*'bâbrek*	бъбрек

kilo	*kilo'gram*	килограм
kilometre	*kilo'metâr*	километър
kindergarten	*'detska gra'dina*	детска градина
king	*kral*	крал
kiosk	*'butka za 'vesnitsi*	будка за вестници
kitchen	*'kuhnya*	кухня
knee	*ko'lyano*	коляно
knife	*nosh*	нож
to know	*znam*	знам

L

label	*eti'ket*	етикет
lady	*'dama*	дама
lake	*'ezero*	езеро
lamb (meat)	*'agneshko*	агнешко
lamp	*'lampa*	лампа
land	*ze'mya*	земя
language	*e'zik*	език
late	*'kâsen*	късен
to laugh	*'smeya se*	смея се
law	*za'kon*	закон
lawyer	*advo'kat*	адвокат
lazy	*mârze'lif*	мързелив
leather	*'kozha*	кожа
left	*lyaf*	ляв
on the left	*na'lyavo*	наляво
leg	*krak*	крак
leisure	*svo'bodno 'vreme*	свободно време
lemon	*li'mon*	лимон
lemonade	*limo'nada*	лимонада
lesson	*u'rok*	урок
letter	*pis'mo*	писмо
letter (of the alphabet)	*'bukva*	буква
lettuce	*ma'rulya*	маруля
library	*biblio'teka*	библиотека
licence	*razre'shitelno*	разрешително

life	*zhi'vot*	живот
to like	*ha'resvam*	харесвам
lipstick	*cher'vilo*	червило
litre	*'litâr*	литър
lobster	*o'mar*	омар
local	*'mesten*	местен
long	*'dâlâk*	дълъг
to look	*'gledam*	гледам
lorry	*kami'on*	камион
to lose	*'gubya*	губя
lost	*iz'guben*	изгубен
lotion	*losi'on*	лосион
lottery	*lo'taria*	лотария
love	*lyu'bof*	любов
luck	*kâs'met*	късмет
luggage	*ba'gash*	багаж
lunch	*'obet*	обед
lung	*byal drop*	бял дроб

M

magazine	*spi'sanie*	списание
mail	*'poshta*	поща
mailbox	*'poshtenska ku'tia*	пощенска кутия
main	*'glaven, 'nay-'vazhen*	главен, най-важен
to make	*'pravya*	правя
make-up	*grim*	грим
man	*mâsh*	мъж
many	*'mnogo*	много
map	*'karta*	карта
March	*mart*	март
margarine	*marga'rin*	маргарин
market	*pa'zar*	пазар
marriage	*zhe'nidba*	женитба
married (man)	*'zhenen*	женен
married (woman)	*o'mâzhena*	омъжена
May	*may*	май

maybe	*'mozhe bi*	може би
meal	*'yadene*	ядене
meat	*me'so*	месо
medicine (prescribed)	*le'karstvo*	лекарство
medicine (science)	*medi'tsina*	медицина
melon	*'pâpesh*	пъпеш
menu	*me'nyu*	меню
message	*sâop'shtenie*	съобщение
metre	*'metâr*	метър
midnight	*polu'nosht*	полунощ
milk	*'pryasno 'mlyako*	прясно мляко
milkshake	*'mlechen sheyk*	млечен шейк
mince	*kay'ma*	кайма
mint	*'menta*	мента
minute	*mi'nuta*	минута
mirror	*ogle'dalo*	огледало
mistake	*'greshka*	грешка
modern	*mo'deren*	модерен
monastery	*manas'tir*	манастир
Monday	*pone'delnik*	понеделник
money	*pa'ri*	пари
month	*'mesets*	месец
monument	*'pametnik*	паметник
moon	*lu'na*	луна
more	*'poveche*	повече
morning	*'sutrin*	сутрин
mosque	*dzha'mia*	джамия
mosquito	*ko'mar*	комар
motel	*mo'tel*	мотел
mother	*'mayka*	майка
motorbike	*moto'pet*	мотопед
motorcycle	*mototsik'let*	мотоциклет
mountain	*plani'na*	планина
moustache	*mus'tatsi*	мустаци
mouth	*us'ta*	уста
movie	*film*	филм
Mr	*gospo'din*	господин
Mrs	*gospo'zha*	госпожа
much	*'mnogo*	много
muscle	*'muskul*	мускул

museum	*mu'zey*	музей
mushroom	*'gâba*	гъба
music	*'muzika*	музика
must	*'tryabva*	трябва
mustard	*gor'chitsa*	горчица
my	*moy*	мой

N

naked	*gol*	гол
name	*'ime*	име
napkin	*sal'fetka*	салфетка
nationality	*natsio'nalnost*	националност
nature	*pri'roda*	природа
nearby	*nab'lizo*	наблизо
necessary	*'nuzhen*	нужен
neck	*vrat*	врат
necklace	*koli'e*	колие
need	*'nuzhda*	нужда
needle	*ig'la*	игла
negative (answer)	*otri'tsatelen*	отрицателен
nephew	*'plemenik*	племенник
nervous	*'nerven*	нервен
network	*'mrezha*	мрежа
never	*'nikoga*	никога
new	*nof*	нов
news	*novi'ni*	новини
newspaper	*'vesnik*	вестник
next	*'sledvasht*	следващ
nice	*pri'yaten*	приятен
niece	*'plemenitsa*	племенница
night	*nosht*	нощ
nightgown	*'noshnitsa*	нощница
nine	*'devet*	девет
nineteen	*devet'nayset*	деветнайсет
ninety	*devede'set*	деветдесет
no	*ne*	не

nobody	*'nikoy*	никой
noisy	*'shumen*	шумен
non-alcoholic	*bezalko'holen*	безалкохолен
nonsense	*'gluposti*	глупости
non-smoker	*nepu'shach*	непушач
noodles	*fi'de*	фиде
noon	*'pladne*	пладне
normal	*nor'malen*	нормален
north	*'sever*	север
northeast	*severo'istok*	североизток
northwest	*severo'zapat*	северозапад
nose	*nos*	нос
note	*be'leshka*	бележка
notebook	*be'lezhnik*	бележник
nothing	*'nishto*	нищо
novel (book)	*ro'man*	роман
November	*no'emvri*	ноември
now	*se'ga*	сега
number	*'nomer*	номер
nun	*mona'hinya*	монахиня
nurse	*medi'tsinska ses'tra*	медицинска сестра
nut (fruit)	*'yatka*	ядка

O

object	*pred'met*	предмет
occasion	*'sluchay*	случай
occupation (profession)	*pro'fesia*	професия
ocean	*oke'an*	океан
o'clock	*cha'sa*	часа
at six o'clock	*f shes cha'sa*	в шест часа
October	*ok'tomvri*	октомври
octopus	*okto'pot*	октопод
offer	*predlo'zhenie*	предложение
often	*'chesto*	често
oil (for cooking)	*'olio*	олио

DICTIONARY

OK	*dob're*	добре
old	*star*	стар
olive	*mas'lina*	маслина
olive oil	*zeh'tin*	зехтин
omelette	*om'let*	омлет
once	*e'din pât*	един път
one	*ed'no*	едно
one-way ticket	*ednopo'sochen bi'let*	еднопосочен билет
onion	*luk*	лук
only	*'samo*	само
to open	*ot'varyam*	отварям
open (not closed)	*ot'voren*	отворен
opening hours	*ra'botno 'vreme*	работно време
opera	*'opera*	опера
operator	*telefo'nist*	телефонист
optician	*op'tik*	оптик
or	*i'li*	или
orange (fruit)	*porto'kal*	портокал
orchard	*o'voshna gra'dina*	овощна градина
order	*ret*	ред
ordinary	*obikno'ven*	обикновен
organization	*organi'zatsia*	организация
original (mind)	*origi'nalen*	оригинален
other	*druk*	друг
our	*nash*	наш
outfit	*ekipi'rofka*	екипировка
outside	*na'vân*	навън
over	*nat*	над
to owe	*dâl'zha*	дължа
own	*'sopstven*	собствен
owner	*'sopstvenik*	собственик
oxygen	*kislo'rot*	кислород
oyster	*'strida*	стрида
ozone	*o'zon*	озон

P

pack of cards	*tes'te 'karti*	тесте карти
packet	*pa'ket*	пакет
page	*'stranitsa*	страница
pain	*'bolka*	болка
paint	*bo'ya*	боя
painter	*hu'dozhnik*	художник
painting	*kar'tina*	картина
pair	*chift*	чифт
pan	*ti'gan*	тиган
pancake	*pala'chinka*	палачинка
pants	*panta'loni*	панталони
paper	*har'tia*	хартия
parcel	*ko'let*	колет
pardon	*izvi'nenie*	извинение
parent	*ro'ditel*	родител
park	*park*	парк
parliament	*parla'ment*	парламент
parsley	*magda'nos*	магданоз
part	*chast*	част
party	*'parti*	парти
passenger	*'pâtnik*	пътник
pasta	*maka'roneni iz'delia*	макаронени изделия
pastry	*slat'kishi*	сладкиши
path	*pâ'teka*	пътека
patient (in hospital)	*patsi'ent*	пациент
to pay	*'plashtam*	плащам
peas	*grah*	грах
peace	*mir*	мир
peach	*'praskova*	праскова
peak	*vrâh*	връх
peanut	*fâs'tâk*	фъстък
pear	*'krusha*	круша
pearl	*'perla*	перла
pedestrian	*peshe'hodets*	пешеходец
pedestrian crossing	*peshe'hodna pâ'teka*	пешеходна пътека
pencil	*mo'lif*	молив

DICTIONARY

peninsula	*polu'ostrof*	полуостров
penknife	*'dzhobno 'noshche*	джобно ножче
people	*'hora*	хора
pepper (spice)	*'cheren pi'per*	черен пипер
pepper (vegetable)	*'chushka*	чушка
per cent	*pro'tsent*	процент
perfect	*sâvâr'shen*	съвършен
performance	*pretstav'lenie*	представление
perfume	*par'fyum*	парфюм
perhaps	*'mozhe bi*	може би
permission	*razre'shenie*	разрешение
person	*cho'vek*	човек
personal	*'lichen*	личен
phone	*tele'fon*	телефон
phonecard	*'fono'karta*	фонокарта
photograph	*'snimka*	снимка
photographer	*foto'graf*	фотограф
piano	*pi'ano*	пиано
picture	*kar'tina*	картина
piece	*par'che*	парче
pill	*'hapche*	хапче
pillow	*vâz'glavnitsa*	възглавница
pilot	*pi'lot*	пилот
pin	*kar'fitsa*	карфица
pineapple	*ana'nas*	ананас
pink	*'rozof*	розов
pizza	*'pitsa*	пица
place	*'myasto*	място
plant (vegetation)	*ras'tenie*	растение
plastic (cup)	*'plasmasof*	пластмасов
plate	*chi'nia*	чиния
platform (railway)	*pe'ron*	перон
play (in theatre)	*pi'esa*	пиеса
to play (games)	*ig'raya*	играя
playground	*ig'rishte*	игрище
pleasure	*udo'volstvie*	удоволствие
plug	*'shtepsel*	щепсел
plum	*'sliva*	слива
pocket	*dzhop*	джоб

poison	*ot'rova*	отрова
police	*po'litsia*	полиция
policeman	*poli'tsay*	полицай
politician	*poli'tik*	политик
poor	*'beden*	беден
popcorn	*'pukanki*	пуканки
popular	*popu'lyaren*	популярен
population	*nase'lenie*	население
pork	*'svinsko (me'so)*	свинско (месо)
port	*pris'tanishte*	пристанище
porter	*porti'er*	портиер
positive	*polo'zhitelen*	положителен
post office	*'poshta*	поща
postbox	*'poshtenska ku'tia*	пощенска кутия
postcard	*'poshtenska 'kartichka*	пощенска картичка
post code	*'poshtenski kot*	пощенски код
poster	*pla'kat*	плакат
postman	*poshta'lyon*	пощальон
pot	*gâr'ne*	гърне
potato	*kar'tof*	картоф
pottery	*grân'charstvo*	грънчарство
pound (sterling)	*'lira*	лира
power	*'sila*	сила
precious	*skâpo'tsenen*	скъпоценен
to prefer	*pretpo'chitam*	предпочитам
prescription	*re'tsepta*	рецепта
present	*po'darâk*	подарък
president	*prezi'dent*	президент
price	*tse'na*	цена
priest	*sve'shtenik*	свещеник
prime-minister	*mi'nistâr-pretse'datel*	министър-председател
prison	*zat'vor*	затвор
prize	*nag'rada*	награда
probably	*vero'yatno*	вероятно
programme	*prog'rama*	програма
pub	*'krâchma*	кръчма
public (service)	*op'shtestven*	обществен
pumpkin	*'tikva*	тиква
pure	*chist*	чист

to put	*'slagam*	слагам
pyjamas	*pi'zhama*	пижама

Q

quality	*'kachestvo*	качество
quantity	*ko'lichestvo*	количество
quarter (1/4)	*'chetvârt*	четвърт
quay	*key*	кей
queen	*tsa'ritsa*	царица
question	*vâp'ros*	въпрос
queue	*o'pashka*	опашка
quickly	*'bârzo*	бързо
quiet	*tih*	тих
be quiet!	*'tiho!*	тихо!
quince	*'dyulya*	дюля
quite	*'dosta*	доста

R

racket (in tennis)	*'tenis ra'keta*	тенис ракета
radio	*'radio*	радио
radish	*'repichka*	репичка
railway	*zhe'leznitsa*	железница
rain	*dâsht*	дъжд
It's raining.	*Va'li dâsht.*	Вали дъжд.
rainbow	*dâ'ga*	дъга
raincoat	*dâzhdo'bran*	дъждобран
raisin	*sta'fida*	стафида
rare	*'ryadâk*	рядък
raspberry	*ma'lina*	малина
raw	*su'rof*	суров

razor	*samobrâs'nachka*	самобръсначка
to reach	*'stigam do*	стигам до
to read	*che'ta*	чета
ready	*go'tof*	готов
receptionist	*adminis'trator*	администратор
recipe	*re'tsepta*	рецепта
recovery	*ozdra'vyavane*	оздравяване
red	*cher'ven*	червен
regular	*re'doven*	редовен
rehearsal	*repe'titsia*	репетиция
relative (kinsman)	*rod'nina*	роднина
to remember	*'pomnya*	помня
to repair	*pop'ravyam*	поправям
report	*dok'lat*	доклад
request	*mol'ba*	молба
to require	*i'ziskvam*	изисквам
research	*pro'uchvane*	проучване
reservation (in a hotel)	*rezer'vatsia*	резервация
reservation (wildlife)	*rezer'vat*	резерват
rest	*po'chifka*	почивка
restaurant	*resto'rant*	ресторант
restroom	*toa'letna*	тоалетна
rib	*reb'ro*	ребро
rice	*o'ris*	ориз
rich	*bo'gat*	богат
to ride (a horse)	*'yazdya*	яздя
right (not left)	*'desen*	десен
right (correct)	*'pravilen*	правилен
ring (on the finger)	*'prâsten*	пръстен
to ring (of phone)	*zvâ'nya*	звъня
to rise (of sun)	*iz'gryavam*	изгрявам
river	*re'ka*	река
road	*pât*	път
roast	*'pecheno (me'so)*	печено (месо)
to rob	*og'rabvam*	ограбвам
robber	*kra'dets*	крадец
rock	*ska'la*	скала
roll	*ru'lo*	руло
rollerblades	*'roleri*	ролери
roller-skates	*'rolkovi 'kânki*	ролкови кънки

roof	*'pokrif*	покрив
room	*'staya*	стая
rope	*vâ'zhe*	въже
rose (flower)	*'roza*	роза
rotten	*razva'len*	развален
rough (of manners)	*grup*	груб
rough (sea)	*'buren*	бурен
round (route)	*obi'kolka*	обиколка
round (shape)	*'krâgâl*	кръгъл
roundabout	*'krâgovo dvi'zhenie*	кръгово движение
route	*marsh'rut*	маршрут
to row (of boat)	*gre'ba*	греба
to ruin	*razru'shavam*	разрушавам
rule	*'pravilo*	правило
to run	*'byagam*	бягам

S

sad	*'tâzhen*	тъжен
safe (not dangerous)	*bezo'pasen*	безопасен
saint	*sve'tets*	светец
salad	*sa'lata*	салата
salary	*zap'lata*	заплата
sale	*pro'dazhba*	продажба
salesperson	*proda'vach*	продавач
salmon (fish)	*'syomga*	сьомга
salt	*sol*	сол
same	*sâsht*	същ
sand	*'pyasâk*	пясък
sandal	*san'dal*	сандал
Saturday	*'sâbota*	събота
sauce	*sos*	сос
saucepan	*'tenzhera*	тенджера
sausage	*kol'bas*	колбас
to save (sb's life)	*spa'syavam*	спасявам
to save (money)	*spes'tyavam*	спестявам
to say	*'kazvam*	казвам

scent	*aro'mat*	аромат
schedule	*raspi'sanie*	разписание
school	*u'chilishte*	училище
science	*na'uka*	наука
science-fiction	*na'uchna fan'tastika*	научна фантастика
scissors	*'nozhitsa*	ножица
scooter	*'skuter*	скутер
screen	*ek'ran*	екран
screwdriver	*ot'verka*	отвертка
scuba-diving	*'gmurkane s akva'lank*	гмуркане с акваланг
sea	*mo're*	море
seafood	*'morska hra'na*	морска храна
seaside	*kray'brezhie*	крайбрежие
seat	*'myasto*	място
seatbelt	*pret'pazen ko'lan*	предпазен колан
to see	*'vizhdam*	виждам
to sell	*pro'davam*	продавам
to send	*is'prashtam*	изпращам
sender	*po'datel*	подател
September	*sep'temvri*	септември
service	*op'sluzhvane*	обслужване
seven	*'sedem*	седем
seventeen	*sedem'nayset*	седемнайсет
seventy	*sedemde'set*	седемдесет
sex (male/female)	*pol*	пол
sex (intercourse)	*seks*	секс
to shake (a bottle)	*ras'klashtam*	разклащам
to shake (with cold)	*tre'perya*	треперя
shampoo	*shampo'an*	шампоан
shape	*'forma*	форма
sharp	*'ostâr*	остър
to shave (a person)	*'brâsna*	бръсна
to shave (oneself)	*'brâsna se*	бръсна се
shaving-cream	*krem za 'brâsnene*	крем за бръснене
she	*tya*	тя
sheet (of paper)	*list har'tia*	лист хартия
sheet (linen)	*char'shaf*	чаршаф
ship	*'korap*	кораб
shirt	*'riza*	риза
shoe	*o'bufka*	обувка

DICTIONARY

shoe polish	*bo'ya za o'bufki*	боя за обувки
shoelace	*'vrâska za o'bufki*	връзка за обувки
shoemaker	*obu'shtar*	обущар
shop	*maga'zin*	магазин
short	*kâs*	къс
shorts	*'kâsi panta'loni*	къси панталони
shoulder	*'ramo*	рамо
shower	*dush*	душ
to shut	*zat'varyam*	затварям
sick	*'bolen*	болен
sights	*zabele'zhitelnosti*	забележителности
silk	*kop'rina*	коприна
silver (metal)	*sreb'ro*	сребро
to sing	*'peya*	пея
singer	*pe'vets*	певец
single (not married – man)	*ne'zhenen*	неженен
single (woman)	*neo'mâzhena*	неомъжена
sister	*ses'tra*	сестра
to sit	*se'dya*	седя
Sit down, please!	*Sed'nete, 'molya!*	Седнете, моля!
six	*shest*	шест
sixteen	*shes'nayset*	шестнайсет
sixty	*shey'set*	шейсет
size (of clothes)	*raz'mer*	размер
size (of shoes)	*'nomer*	номер
skates	*'kânki*	кънки
skateboard	*'skeyt'bort*	скейтборд
to ski	*'karam ski*	карам ски
skin	*'kozha*	кожа
skirt	*po'la*	пола
sky	*ne'be*	небе
sledge	*shey'na*	шейна
to sleep	*spya*	спя
sleeping-bag	*'spalen chu'val*	спален чувал
sleeper	*'spalen va'gon*	спален вагон
sleeve	*râ'kaf*	ръкав
slope	*sklon*	склон
slow	*'baven*	бавен
small	*'malâk*	малък
smart	*'umen*	умен

smell	*miriz'ma*	миризма
smile	*us'mifka*	усмивка
smoke	*'pushek*	пушек
to smoke	*'pusha*	пуша
smuggle	*kontra'banda*	контрабанда
snail	*'ohlyuf*	охлюв
snake	*zmi'a*	змия
sneakers	*mara'tonki*	маратонки
snow	*snyak*	сняг
It's snowing.	*Va'li snyak.*	Вали сняг.
soap	*sa'pun*	сапун
society	*opshtest'vo*	общество
sock	*kâs cho'rap*	къс чорап
somebody	*'nyakoy*	някой
something	*'neshto*	нещо
sometimes	*po'nyakoga*	понякога
son	*sin*	син
song	*'pesen*	песен
soon	*'skoro*	скоро
sore throat	*vâspa'leno 'gârlo*	възпалено гърло
sorry: to be sorry	*sâzha'lyavam*	съжалявам
sound	*zvuk*	звук
soup	*'supa*	супа
sour	*'kisel*	кисел
south	*yuk*	юг
southeast	*yugo'istok*	югоизток
southwest	*yugo'zapat*	югозапад
souvenir	*suve'nir*	сувенир
spare (part)	*re'zervna chast*	резервна част
to speak	*go'vorya*	говоря
spectacles	*ochi'la*	очила
speed	*'skorost*	скорост
to spend (time)	*pre'karvam*	прекарвам
to spend (money)	*'harcha*	харча
spice	*pot'prafka*	подправка
spinach	*spa'nak*	спанак
spine	*grâb'nak*	гръбнак
spoon	*lâ'zhitsa*	лъжица
sport	*sport*	спорт
sportsman	*spor'tist*	спортист

spring (season)	*'prolet*	пролет
square (in town)	*plo'shtat*	площад
stadium	*stadi'on*	стадион
stage (in theatre)	*'stsena*	сцена
stairs	*'stâlbishte*	стълбище
stamp	*'poshtenska 'marka*	пощенска марка
to stand	*sto'ya*	стоя
star	*zvez'da*	звезда
station	*'gara*	гара
steak	*bif'tek*	бифтек
to steal	*kra'da*	крада
steep	*'strâmen*	стръмен
step	*'stâpka*	стъпка
stew	*yah'nia*	яхния
stocking	*'dâlâk cho'rap*	дълъг чорап
stomach	*sto'mah*	стомах
stomachache	*'bolki f sto'maha*	болки в стомаха
stone	*'kamâk*	камък
stop	*'spirka*	спирка
story	*'raskas*	разказ
stranger	*nepoz'nat*	непознат
strawberry	*'yagoda*	ягода
street	*'ulitsa*	улица
striped	*ra'iran*	раиран
strong	*'silen*	силен
to study	*'ucha*	уча
stupid	*'glupaf*	глупав
substance	*veshtest'vo*	вещество
subway	*'podles*	подлез
subway (underground)	*met'ro*	метро
success	*us'peh*	успех
sugar	*'zahar*	захар
suggestion	*predlo'zhenie*	предложение
suit (set of clothes)	*kos'tyum*	костюм
suitcase	*'kufar*	куфар
summer	*'lyato*	лято
sun	*'slântse*	слънце
to sunbathe	*pe'ka se na 'slântse*	пека се на слънце
sunburn	*ten*	тен
Sunday	*ne'delya*	неделя

sunglasses	*'slânchevi ochi'la*	слънчеви очила
sunrise	*'izgref*	изгрев
sunset	*'zales*	залез
sunshine	*'slâncheva svetli'na*	слънчева светлина
supermarket	*'super'market*	супермаркет
supper	*ve'cherya*	вечеря
supporter	*pod'drâzhnik*	поддръжник
to suppose	*pretpo'lagam*	предполагам
sure	*'siguren*	сигурен
surname	*fa'milno 'ime*	фамилно име
surprise	*izne'nada*	изненада
survivor	*otse'lyal*	оцелял
sweater	*pu'lover*	пуловер
sweet	*'sladâk*	сладък
to swim	*'pluvam*	плувам
swimming	*'pluvane*	плуване
swimming-pool	*'pluven ba'seyn*	плувен басейн
to switch on	*'fklyuchvam*	включвам
to switch off	*is'klyuchvam*	изключвам
syrup	*si'rop*	сироп

T

table	*'masa*	маса
tailor	*shi'vach*	шивач
to take off (clothes)	*sâb'licham*	събличам
to take off (plane)	*iz'litam*	излитам
tall	*vi'sok*	висок
tap (of sink)	*kran*	кран
taste	*fkus*	вкус
tax	*'danâk*	данък
tea	*chay*	чай
to teach	*obu'chavam*	обучавам
teacher	*u'chitel*	учител
team	*od'bor*	отбор
telegram	*tele'grama*	телеграма
telephone	*tele'fon*	телефон

television	*tele'vizia*	телевизия
to tell	*'kazvam*	казвам
temperature	*tempera'tura*	температура
ten	*'deset*	десет
tennis	*'tenis*	тенис
tent	*pa'latka*	палатка
terrace	*te'rasa*	тераса
terrible	*u'zhasen*	ужасен
terrific	*stra'hoten*	страхотен
textbook	*u'chebnik*	учебник
thank you!	*blagoda'rya!*	благодаря!
theatre	*te'atâr*	театър
their	*'tehen*	техен
there	*tam*	там
they	*te*	те
thin	*'tânâk*	тънък
thing	*'neshto*	нещо
to think	*'mislya*	мисля
thirsty	*'zhaden*	жаден
thirteen	*tri'nayset*	тринайсет
thirty	*'triyset*	трийсет
thousand	*hi'lyada*	хиляда
three	*tri*	три
throat	*'gârlo*	гърло
to throw	*'hvârlyam*	хвърлям
thumb	*'palets*	палец
Thursday	*chet'vârtâk*	четвъртък
ticket	*bi'let*	билет
tights	*chorapo'gashnik*	чорапогащник
time	*'vreme*	време
timetable	*raspi'sanie*	разписание
tired	*umo'ren*	уморен
title (of a book)	*zag'lavie*	заглавие
toast	*pre'pechen hlyap*	препечен хляб
tobacco	*tyu'tyun*	тютюн
today	*dnes*	днес
toe	*prâst na kra'ka*	пръст на крака
together	*'zaedno*	заедно
toilet (WC)	*toa'letna*	тоалетна
tomato	*do'mat*	домат

tomorrow	*'utre*	утре
tonight	*do'vechera*	довечера
tooth	*zâp*	зъб
toothache	*zâbo'bol*	зъбобол
toothbrush	*'chetka za 'zâbi*	четка за зъби
toothpaste	*'pasta za 'zâbi*	паста за зъби
torch	*fe'nerche*	фенерче
to touch	*do'kosvam*	докосвам
tour	*obi'kolka*	обиколка
tourism	*tu'rizâm*	туризъм
tourist	*tu'rist*	турист
towel	*hav'lia*	хавлия
tower	*'kula*	кула
town	*grat*	град
toy	*ig'rachka*	играчка
trade	*târgo'via*	търговия
traffic	*dvi'zhenie*	движение
traffic lights	*sveto'far*	светофар
tragedy	*tra'gedia*	трагедия
train	*vlak*	влак
tram	*tram'vay*	трамвай
to travel	*pâ'tuvam*	пътувам
traveller	*'pâtnik*	пътник
traveller's cheque	*'pâtnicheski chek*	пътнически чек
treasure	*sâk'rovishte*	съкровище
tree	*dâr'vo*	дърво
trouble	*bespo'koystvo*	безпокойство
trousers	*panta'lon*	панталон
trout	*pâs'târva*	пъстърва
truck	*kami'on*	камион
true	*'veren*	верен
Tuesday	*'ftornik*	вторник
twelve	*dva'nayset*	дванайсет
twenty	*'dvayset*	двайсет
twice	*dva 'pâti*	два пъти
twin	*bliz'nak*	близнак
two	*dve*	две
tyre	*'guma*	гума

Dictionary

U

ugly	*'grozen*	грозен
umbrella	*cha'dâr*	чадър
uncle	*'chicho*	чичо
under	*pot*	под
underwear	*be'lyo*	бельо
unhappy	*ne'shtasten*	нещастен
university	*universi'tet*	университет
until	*do*	до
upstairs	*na 'gornia e'tash*	на горния етаж
urgent	*'speshen*	спешен
use	*upo'treba*	употреба
useful	*po'lezen*	полезен
useless	*bespo'lezen*	безполезен
usually	*obikno'veno*	обикновено

V

vacant	*svo'boden*	свободен
to vaccinate	*vaksi'niram*	ваксинирам
vacuum cleaner	*prahosmu'kachka*	прахосмукачка
valley	*doli'na*	долина
valuable	*'tsenen*	ценен
van	*kara'vana*	каравана
vegetable	*zelen'chuk*	зеленчук
vegetarian	*vegetari'anets*	вегетарианец
vehicle	*pre'vozno 'sretstvo*	превозно средство
vein	*'vena*	вена
velvet	*kadi'fe*	кадифе
very	*'mnogo*	много
vessel	*sât*	съд
vet	*veteri'naren 'lekar*	ветеринарен лекар
victim	*'zhertva*	жертва
victory	*po'beda*	победа

view	*'izglet*	изглед
village	*'selo*	село
vinegar	*o'tset*	оцет
violin	*tsi'gulka*	цигулка
visa	*'viza*	виза
visit	*pose'shtenie*	посещение
volunteer	*dobro'volets*	доброволец
voyage	*pâ'tuvane po mo're*	пътуване по море

W

waist	*krâst*	кръст
to wait	*'chakam*	чакам
waiter	*servi'tyor*	сервитьор
waiting-room	*cha'kalnya*	чакалня
waitress	*servi'tyorka*	сервитьорка
walk	*ras-'hotka*	разходка
wall	*ste'na*	стена
wallet	*port'feyl*	портфейл
walnut	*'oreh*	орех
to want	*'iskam*	искам
war	*voy'na*	война
wardrobe	*garde'rop*	гардероб
warm	*'topâl*	топъл
warning	*preduprezh'denie*	предупреждение
watch (timepiece)	*cha'sovnik*	часовник
to watch	*'gledam*	гледам
water	*vo'da*	вода
waterfall	*vodo'pat*	водопад
watermelon	*'dinya*	диня
waterproof	*nepromo'kaem*	непромокаем
wave	*vâl'na*	вълна
way	*pât*	път
we	*'nie*	ние
weak	*slap*	слаб
weapon	*o'râzhie*	оръжие
weather	*'vreme*	време

weather forecast	*prog'noza za 'vremeto*	прогноза за времето
to weave	*tâ'ka*	тъка
wedding	*'svadba*	сватба
Wednesday	*'sryada*	сряда
week	*'sedmitsa*	седмица
weekend	*u'ikend*	уикенд
weight	*teg'lo*	тегло
to welcome	*pos'reshtam*	посрещам
well (not bad)	*dob're*	добре
west	*'zapat*	запад
wet	*'vlazhen*	влажен
what	*kak'vo*	какво
wheel	*kole'lo*	колело
wheelchair	*inva'lidna ko'lichka*	инвалидна количка
when	*ko'ga*	кога
where	*kâ'de*	къде
which	*koy*	кой
while	*doka'to*	докато
white	*byal*	бял
who	*koy*	кой
whose	*chiy*	чий
why	*za'shto*	защо
wide	*shi'rok*	широк
widow	*vdo'vitsa*	вдовица
widower	*vdo'vets*	вдовец
wife	*sâp'ruga*	съпруга
wild	*dif*	див
wildlife	*'divi zhi'votni*	диви животни
will (shall)	*shte*	ще
to win	*pe'chelya*	печеля
wind	*'vyatâr*	вятър
window	*pro'zorets*	прозорец
windy	*vetro'vit*	ветровит
wine	*'vino*	вино
winter	*'zima*	зима
wiper (of a car)	*chis'tachka*	чистачка
with	*s(âs)*	с(ъс)
without	*bes*	без
witness	*svi'detel*	свидетел
woman	*zhe'na*	жена
wool	*'vâlna*	вълна